MW00804460

VENICE
ART AND HISTORY

VENICE
ART AND HISTORY

Lorenza Smith

arsenale et editrice

VENICE
ART AND HISTORY

Text by
Lorenza Smith

The author would like to thank
for their precious collaboration:
Flavia Destefanis
Ferne Mele
Triada Samaras

© Arsenale Editrice 2011

First Edition
January 2011

First Reprint
October 2012

Printed in Italy by
EBS Editoriale Bortolazzi-Stei (Verona)

Arsenale Editore Srl
Via Monte Comun, 40
37057 San Giovanni Lupatoto (Verona)
www.arsenale.it

All rights reserved. No part of this publication
may be reproduced, stored in a retrievial
system, or transmitted in any form
or by any means without prior permission
of the Publisher.

ISBN 978 88 7743 349 7

SUMMARY

INTRODUCTION

Alter Venetia mundus
Venezia is another world

(Francesco Petrarca, 1304-1347)

A combination of particularly favorable natural factors, together with human willpower and intelligence, helped to create Venice, a city destined to remain without equal in the world. For this reason, Venice was worthy of a supernatural inception, the date of which was selected precisely as the celebration of the Annunciation (25th March) 421 AD. The elaborate, self-celebratory legend of the city came to be superimposed on the historical truths of the city's evolution.

In reality, at this time, the area from which Venice emerged was made up of unhealthy marshland where the poor sustained their livelihood with fishing and the production of salt. It was only around the end of the 6th century that the populations of the surrounding Roman province, called *Venetia*, spurred by the threat of barbarian invasions, slowly began to establish themselves upon the lagoon. The area then became part of the Eastern or Byzantine Roman Empire, under the control of Constantinople but directly answerable to the local authorities in Ravenna, whose influence over Venice was highly significant.

The new inhabitants of the lagoon had to deal with a challenging natural environment which they managed to control only through a constant struggle. Initially Venice was merely a collection of hundreds of little muddy islands, punctuated with marshes and flooded by the fierce action of the waves. From the 13th century onwards, the city became organized around sixty parishes. Each was defined, corresponding to an island, with its own church, a few town houses and houses, a market and a little port with a small shipyard. The islands were connected by ferries or by simple walkways which, over time, became wooden bridges, later replaced by stone bridges. Each island was considered an organism in itself that within the unity of the archipelago, constituted a single territory answerable to one government initially presided over by the first Doge Angelo Partecipazio. By the 9th century, this government had become almost independent of Ravenna, laying the foundations for the constitution of the Republic.

Several factors led to a rapid growth to Venice's sphere of influence and power: its geographical position at the crucial meeting point in the Mediterranean between the trade routes of northern Europe and those of the Orient; its skilful exploitation of natural resources, the most valuable of which was salt; the efficient organisation of its merchant navy and armed fleet, which ensured the protection of ships from Byzantium, thus obtaining important concessions from Constantinople; and its participation in the Crusades and the active diplomatic network that was created. Thus Venice became the point of reference for the interests of many countries.

Facing page,
Perspective view of Venice.
*Castello del Buonconsiglio
in Trento.*

In order to protect its trade routes and ships from competitors and pirate attacks and to maintain its commercial advantages within the Mediterranean, Venice engaged in a series of wars, creating an empire through the conquest of surrounding territories.

At the height of its expansion, the empire extended from Bergamo and Brescia to the entire Dalmatian coast to as far away as the coasts of Greece, including those of Corfu, part of the Peloponnese, Crete and Cyprus. The Byzantine roots of Venice's cultural and artistic development merged harmoniously with the later Roman heritage left by its first inhabitants. Witness to this are some precious examples of the city's architecture, such as the palaces on the Grand Canal, whose long loggias exhibit the same structural solutions found on Roman villas in the inland areas.

For almost five hundred years, until the 13th century, formal Byzantine elements continued to populate the campi (squares), the calli (streets), and the banks of the canals, leaving traces of fine workmanship especially in the religious buildings such as the cathedrals of Torcello and Murano. The most grandiose accomplishment was the St. Mark's basilica which, like the church of the Holy Apostles in Constantinople upon which it was based, featured a Greek cross plan, and majestic cupolas that surmount wide arches punctuated with small windows.

In the 14th century, after the Crusades and the reappearance of the Western world on the Mediterranean, which had for centuries been dominated by the advancement of Islam, Venice had almost reached its definitive size. With its 120,000 inhabitants (a number twice as large as the current population) Venice became one of the most important cities of Europe, a transit point for almost all the freight transported in the known world of the time: spices from the Far East, grain from the southern Mediterranean and wool from England. Thanks to the flourishing industries which had developed in the territories of Venice, in particular in the mainland areas, the trader-traveler was furthermore able to find a wide range of products: from silk and woolen cloth to glass, from ornate leather to jewelry.

In the 14th century, Gothic style began to redefine the city: acute arches, pinnacles, towering columns and fretwork façades to flourish for almost 150 years, leaving an imprint that still characterizes the appearance of Venice today. The new style was introduced by the Mendicant monastic order, carriers of new trends from the north. The most impressive examples can be found in the imposing churches of SS Giovanni e Paolo as well as S. Maria Gloriosa dei Frari: a style that quickly spread to domestic architecture and urban furnishing.

At the time of the flourishing of the Renaissance style in Florence, Venice, with its links to the north of Europe and the East due to its commercial interests, continued to build in the Gothic style which, over time, assumed a characteristic aspect which was called *gotico fiorito*. This style was distinguished by the detail of the volutes and by the lines and patterns reminiscent of lacework. The highest expression of this architectural language, so deeply entrenched in the urban fabric, is undoubtedly the Doge's Palace.

It was only after the mid-fifteenth century that the Renaissance concepts of order and proportion derived from classical legacy, also began to appear in Venice setting the stage for the work of Mauro Codussi, an architect who was well-read in the instruction of Leon Battista Alberti and the principles of Tuscan Humanism. Historical accounts narrate the wonderment that Codussi's church of S. Michele in Isola caused in 1469 when the extensive scaffolding was dismantled. The white Istrian stone façade was characterized by the delicate play of ashlar, the purity of the lines, and the central lunette, and its reflection in the waters of the lagoon was an amazing view.

In the following years Codussi was involved

in religious and civil projects: Palazzo Vendramin Calergi on the Grand Canal is the finest example. His constructions presented sophisticated architectural solutions in a very different style from the other great architect of the time, Pietro Lombardo, with whom he had worked together on a number of projects.

In fact, Lombardo's passion focused on the richness of the chromatic scale and his research into plastic decorative elements rather than on architectural structure as evidenced in the church of S. Maria dei Miracoli and the Palazzo Dario.

Color and light have always been intrinsic to Venetian art, both in the sphere of architecture and in the art of painting. One can find examples of this relating to the latter in the majestic style of Giovanni Bellini who, while remaining attached to local tradition, was able to assimilate the formal Renaissance principles overtaking the Gothic style (dominant until mid-fifteenth century), and contributing in a decisive manner to the foundation of the great Venetian school of painting. Bellini's art, with its demure and solemn Madonnas and brightly-colored altarpieces, is infused with religious sentiment, poetry and pantheistic spirituality. In his paintings, light radiates outwards from within, evoking a sense of mystical transcendence. His style is very different from that of the two great narrative artists of Venetian life, Vittore Carpaccio and especially his brother Gentile Bellini, whose paintings like the *Procession in Saint Mark's Square,* bring late 15th century Venice

Imaginary reconstruction of early Medieval Venice, Marciana Library.

to life by documenting the city itself, its traditions, routines and the faces of those who ruled and lived there.

From the Medieval Ages onwards, the term *scuola* was used in Venice to refer to confraternities whose members were dedicated to pious devotion and charity; among this group, many were professionals and focused on encouraging common devotion and reciprocal support. Not all of the confraternities were, however, formed on the basis of their members' profession. Many were founded to serve immigrant communities who had settled in Venice. It is also interesting to note that the term *scuola* also was used to describe Venetian synagogues.

By the mid-sixteenth century, six of these confraternities were categorized as Scuole Grandi, while the number of Scuole Piccole had grown to over a hundred. The function of these institutions was to provide relief from poverty and social isolation and by the eighteenth century, their number had more than doubled. The members of such institutions were essentially able to count on a sort of insurance against destitution and isolation. These organisms additionally found a valuable narrator in Vittore Carpaccio, a painter whose creativity and command of perspective enabled him to bring ancient legends to life. The most fascinating example of his work is the *Life of St. Ursula* in which the characters wear elaborate costumes of the period: the setting recalls a fantastical Codussian Venice.

The 16th century began with the extraordinary character of Giorgione who revolutionized traditional painting and is considered, thanks to his innovative technique, the first modern painter of Venice. In his evocative and poetic compositions, figures are depicted blending into the idyllic landscapes by which they are surrounded. Giorgione's career was cut short by an early death but his artistic legacy is considerable. Many of his pictures are a literary inspiration, extremely rare in a world in which religious subjects dominated artistic production. Giorgione is perhaps best known for the mystery with which he infused his paintings, best exemplified by *The Tempest.*

Giorgione is also known to have been Titian's teacher, collaborating with his pupil on various commissions to eventually dominate the art world of the lagoon for the majority of the sixteenth century. Reassuming the tradition of the Venetian chromatic scale and combining this with a formal and compositional language formed on the basis of Giorgione's teaching, Titian managed to confer on his paintings a new expressive force. The innovative dynamism of the *Assumption of the Virgin* at S. Maria Gloriosa dei Frari and the unprecedented figural relationships found in the Pesaro Altarpiece demonstrate how Titian came to reject the strict order and rigidity of the Byzantine tradition adopted by Bellini and his contemporaries. The solemn composure of his characters, originating from a learned interpretation of the classic balance, infused his depictions of sensual feminine beauty in paintings such as *Sacred and Profane Love* and the *Venus of Urbino.* These canvasses show wide color planes that over the years would flake and fall away to leave the shady appearance of the later dramatic pieces (for example *The Martyrdom of St. Lawrence* or *The Pietà*). Titian became one of the most renowned artists of his time, becoming an official painter of the Republic, a title that had been previously held by Bellini. Titian's patrons included the ruling figures of Italy and Europe who commissioned from him portraits of acute psychological introspection and communicative power, most famously exemplified by his equestrian portrait of the Holy Roman Emperor and King of Spain Charles V.

The great Venetian 1500s progressed with Paolo Veronese who arrived a youngster in the city midway through the century. His unusual palette of delicate and bright colors, haziness and vibrancy, enabled him to create fantastic architectural works, light perspectives and spectacular biblical scenes. The attention with which he interpreted the movement of the drapery of the rich brocades and heavy silks in paintings such as the *The Feast in the House of Levi* or *The Family of Darius before Alexander* were particularly admired. Veronese masterly converted ancient stories to a contemporary setting, receiving vast and important commissions such as the decoration of the ceilings of Doge's Palace. Equally impressive were the fresco decoration of Villa Maser for the Barbaros, one of the many patrician families who would build important residences on the mainland.

A contemporary of Veronese who had a very different temperament was Jacopo Tintoretto, an artist who left a deep mark on the vibrant Venetian landscape in the second half of the 16th century. He was the son of a cloth dyer (in Venetian *tintor* from whence his name is derived) who, unlike Titian and Veronese, had no links or relationships with important patrons. In order to secure his commissions he resorted to unusual strategies such as in the case of the Scuola di San Rocco where he decorated the entire interior space with a series of paintings executed over a twenty-five year period.

These were the times of the Counter-Reformation and art distanced itself from Renaissance tranquility, introducing representations closer to reality and, as such, more realistic and thus more easily understood by the masses. During the course of his career, Tintoretto became aware of this spirit, which we can see for example in his *Miracle of the Slave* (Gallerie dell'Accademia), or the *Last Supper* in the church of S. Giorgio Maggiore. These paintings are characterized by daring perspectives and an internal dynamism, and are noteworthy for their volumes and the positioning of the individual figures. Tintoretto's use of light also provided a fundamental unifying tool for his compositions.

At the beginning of the 16th century, the Republic of Venice was one of the most important States of Europe and its ambitious ex-

pansionist policies began to impact the interests of many. As a result, in 1508, the Papacy, the Empire, France, and several minor States united as the League of Cambrai with the shared aim of halting Venice. Given the disproportionate military advantage the League held over Venice, it was easy to expect that the Republic would be defeated. Nonetheless Venice, using all of its military might, activating the network of its most competent diplomats, and exploiting the strategic weaknesses of the enemy, emerged victorious and managed to maintain almost all of its territory intact. However, this victory, together with the decisive contribution made at the battle of Lepanto in 1571, did not halt the course of history: the formation of great national States and new geographical discoveries were radically changing the global geopolitical scene, eventually relegating Venice to a marginal position. Obviously, this was a gradual process and the Republic continued to exercise its role on the international scene, even if its essential presence within the balance of world commercial traffic was slowly beginning to disappear.

Overcoming the difficulties caused by the great sacrifices of war, Venice needed, as never before, to present a strong image to the world. The arrival of Jacopo Sansovino from Rome in 1527 proved highly providential in this respect. In 1529, he was appointed as the state architect, supervising all work on the basilica and other public buildings.

In this manner he came to assume the most important public role in the field of construction. Among the work that he received was the restructuring of Saint Mark's Square, a project he undertook according to the directives of a government that wished to establish a civic center that would fully represent the glory of the Republic. This work of Sansovino introduced a Roman style to Venice that was appropriate to the highly symbolic value of the place, but at the same time contemporary with the individual buildings and with their perspective planning. In addition to the

Facing page,
the church of the Redentore
by Andrea Palladio expresses
a sense of severe
magnificence through
its façade inspired
by classical temples.

projects he completed at the Doge's Palace and the Basilica, Sansovino also built in the vicinity of Saint Mark's Square the Zecca (the Mint), the Libreria, and the Loggetta at the foot of the bell tower and made various changes to pre-existing structures. Furthermore he designed many other public and private buildings as well as religious structures, such as the churches of S. Francesco della Vigna and S. Geminiano.

During a period in which the Serenissima's certainties fluctuated, it was important to give the people a sense of trust through the expansion and enhancement of the historical landmarks of the city: Saint Mark's Square and Rialto. Sansovino was appointed to construct a number of buildings for the latter, the commercial center of Venice, and later, in 1587, Antonio Da Ponte won the contest for the construction of the famous Rialto bridge. By 1515, following a devastating fire, Antonio Scarpagnino was entrusted with the reconstruction of the market.

By contrast, the government resisted accepting the overly modern project for the Rialto bridge of Andrea Palladio, the architect who, in the centuries to come, would have more followers in the world than any other architect, from England to the United States. Already famous in Veneto because of his villas and public buildings, Palladio was almost fifty years old when, in 1560, he began to work in Venice, initially summoned by monastic orders for S. Giorgio Maggiore and Convento della Carità. One of his masterpieces was the church of the Redentore built by the Senate of Venice as a vow to Christ. The hope was that this work would liberate the city from one of the most terrible plagues in the history of Venice (1576) which devastated the population, reducing it to almost a third of its size prior to the epidemic. The white façades of his churches, like the churches of S. Giorgio Maggiore and the Zitelle, are characterized by a rigorous structure in which pure geometrical shapes intersect, and bring to mind the structures of classical temples with their columns and gables. The interiors were also inspired by a solemn classic style, filled with a transcendental harmony of solids and voids punctuated at intervals by external light. Palladio's buildings always communicate with the surrounding area in a close relationship between architecture and nature, a feature he incorporated into his Venetian project, finding vast panoramas for his churches built directly on the waters of the lagoon.

The 17th century in Venice began in a different way compared with the other great European cities that underwent radical and profound urban changes. The peculiar structure of the city allowed the spreading of the Baroque style in a completely original way, which was applied according to demand. Baldassarre Longhena was the architect who was best able to combine the requirements of Baroque *grandeur* with the features of the city in the construction of the basilica of Madonna della Salute. The building was erected as a vow taken in 1630 by the Senate to the Madonna to request liberation from another devastating plague which was annihilating its citizens. The Republic designated a large area on the lagoon facing the basin of Saint Mark's, precisely at the point where the Grand Canal begins, choosing an extraordinary location in which to place the new structure. The instructions were clear: the church was to become a symbol of the rebirth of Venice. Longhena knew how to fulfill the request for magnificence: by building a large structure with a central plan overarched by a semispherical cupola, supported by large spiral volutes. Despite its imposing appearance, the building was assimilated harmoniously into Venetian tradition with its simplicity and measured balance among the elements.

The state of painting in the 17th century did not match the heights reached by architecture. Artistic production, dominated by the great figures of the previous century, had lost all spirit and creativity, so much so that it was not even possible to speak of a true Venetian

school of painting at this time. Within the city, the most interesting painters were foreigners such as the Roman, Domenico Fetti, the German, Johan Liss, and the Genoese, Bernardo Strozzi. It was furthermore peculiar that Venetian painting had undergone such an about turn when so many great foreign artists such as Rubens, Velasquez and Van Dyck took their inspiration precisely from the Venetian masters.

At the beginning of the 18th century, Venice was still one of the greatest Italian States but was heading towards a gradual downsizing. The government remained essentially unchanged in its constitution: power was in the hands of the aristocratic oligarchy while the population remained completed excluded from political life. Despite a widespread awareness of a general decline, the Republic continued to go about its business, appearing almost to be in a state of denial about reality. Ceremonies, processions, regattas and carnivals continued to animate the streets and canals of Venice, while the patricians enjoyed parties, banquets and balls at their luxurious homes. The 18th century was also a time of the theater: dozens of theaters thrived, and the most important comedy writer was Carlo Goldoni, with his *pièce* which described with indulgent irony Venetian life during that time.

This 18th century activity is also reflected in the construction undertaken with numerous private commissions (including Palazzo Grassi designed by the architect Giorgio Massari), and especially with the transformation of many churches, notably Maddalena (a work by Tommaso Temanza), S. Barnaba, S. Maria della Pietà and S. Rocco.

Venetian painting also seemed to discover energy thanks to the artists that reached success at the European level. Canaletto was one of the most famous painters of the time: his brilliant scenes of the city were bought by travelers from all over the world during their stay in Venice, an obligatory stopover on the *Grand Tour*. His paintings' panoramic views span Saint Mark's Square, the Grand Canal, the campi (squares) and canals of the city, and a particular love for architecture and for the human form is evident, accomplished with great attention to detail.

Amongst the many landscape painters of this time, the artist Francesco Guardi stands out, despite the fact that was a lot less successful than Canaletto. His landscapes and his *capricci* are characterized by hazy surroundings and are set within a rich atmosphere revealing a delicate sensitivity that is almost romantic in its style, quite differently from the paintings of Canaletto.

The artist Giambattista Piazzetta on the other hand was interested in other subject matters and dedicated himself predominantly to religious themes. In Piazzetta's works the usual vibrant range of Venetian colors was replaced by the use of light and shade effects, in which light is restored with strokes of white or blue, as demonstrated by his altarpieces which can be seen in various churches of the city.

But the last great artist of the Serenissima was without doubt Giambattista Tiepolo, who was admired and praised for his virtuosity and inventive capacity. His grandiose frescoes are bathed in a warm sunlight in which angels, horses, saints, biblical and mythological story characters, amongst others, cavort, circling joyfully. In a celebration of carefully executed foreshortening, movements and flowing drapes, the brilliance and profusion of the colors brings special vigor to the fantastic tales. Among Tiepolo's great painting masterpieces, the frescoes in Palazzo Labia and Ca' Rezzonico stand out, followed by the numerous altarpieces that grace the most beautiful churches of the city, including the church of SS Apostoli and S. Alvise.

At the end of the 18th century, Venice, which had adhered for years to a forced neutrality, had conceded many of its Mediterranean lands, and no political force seemed able to halt the decline. Attempts at reform – many of which took place around the mid 18th cen-

tury – were lost within palace games or met with an impenetrable wall of consolidated bureaucracy dating back thousands of years. When Napoleon arrived with his army on 12th May 1797, he not only found no obstacles on his way, but he even lead a number of citizens to believe that he was the forerunner of new ideas of freedom from post revolutionary France. In this way, the city made the transition from thousands of years of stability, autonomy and well-being to a difficult era marked by alternating domination by the French and the Austrians. Among the great changes that the Napoleonic government imposed on the city was the suppression of religious corporations, churches and scuole,

causing incalculable damage to the city's spiritual and economic fabric.

The artistic revival of the 18th century experienced its final triumph with the great sculptor Antonio Canova, whose Neoclassic style took him to Rome, a fertile ground for this language. From where he influenced the European sculpture scene for many years to come. But Neoclassicism had also taken hold in Venice where its spread continued until the 1830s. A stylistic aspect that developed in particular was interior decorating, first applied to the Royal Palace and to La Fenice Opera House, rebuilt after the fire of 1836. Following this, after a historical-romantic period, Venetian artists turned predominantly

The Neoclassical pavilion called Coffee House was conceived within an urban structure commissioned by Napoleon.

Preceding pages,
La Fenice Opera House
was destroyed by fire for
the second time in 1996,
only to be rebuilt exactly
as it once was.

to genre painting, creating representations free from all symbolic value that re-proposed reality as it was.

With the Congress of Vienna (1815), Venice was annexed to the Habsburg Empire (which changed the city's manufacturing and commercial activities). Venice was annexed to the Kingdom of Italy in 1866, five years after the unification of Italy. The city continued to experience difficult conditions but the new authorities committed themselves to important urban changes that radically modified an area that for centuries had remained unchanged.

Painters of particular interest for art history who were active in Venice during those years included Giacomo Favretto, initially linked to the 18th century tradition. His style was reminiscent of Tiepolescan tonality and later he took up representations of everyday moments in city life. Other notable artists are Luigi Nono, a typical example of the realist Venetian school who, in his first work, captured the simple and melancholic existence of the people, later devoting himself to painting using more vibrant colors; and Ettore Tito, who shifted away from naturalistic experiences to arrive, at the end of the century, at a fluid painting style, rich in dynamic perspective which brought him a number of interesting public commissions. Alessandro Milesi latched on to the tradition of portrait painting with his own personal style while also dedicating himself to general scenes using Venetian subjects. The work of the landscaper Guglielmo Ciardi was on the other hand characterized by great freshness and skillful chromatic play. The wish not to remain isolated and to participate actively in both Italian and European cultural life motivated a group of Venetian intellectuals to establish the Venice Biennale in 1895. This was Italy's first international art exhibition, and continues to date, with its wide variety of exhibitions ranging from visual arts, to theater, to architecture, to dance, to music and to cinema, making the city on the lagoon one of the most important cultural centers.

Parallel to the Biennale, which presented an already established body of art (or, in any case, one that was tied to tradition), the activity at Ca' Pesaro became increasingly known in the first quarter of the 20th century. Ca' Pesaro was a sort of exhibition space that soon became a place of international cultural exchange, brought alive by an aesthetic flavor centered on all that was new and, at the time, revolutionary.

Featured artists included Gino Rossi, whose work is similar to that of the French *fauves* and *nabis* movements, with elements and color inspired by Gauguin; Arturo Martini, who interpreted Nordic Symbolism and Expressionism in plastic form, preferring plaster, terracotta and ceramics for his sculptures carved with a graphic sign that at times brought him close to Futuristic painting; and Felice Casorati, the most cultured and well-known artist, whose paintings, permeated with mystery and immersed in an imaginary light, appeared linked to the Symbolist matrix. Playing a fundamental role within Venetian culture were also the exhibitions of the Bevilacqua La Masa Foundation, which still remains an important reference point for young artists. The artists Pizzinato, Santomaso and Vedova started to exhibit in 1940, later becoming members of the New Front of Arts. In the fifties, a number of the younger artists working in Venice such as Tancredi, De Luigi, Morandis and Finzi began to take an interest in Spacialism. A more solitary path was followed away from the lyrical abstractionism of Music; while Virgilio Guidi spent a large part of the century contributing to the magic use of light so typical of Venetian painting.

In the last forty years of the 20th century, three artists in Venice achieved international fame: Emilio Vedova, Fabrizio Plessi and Maurizio Pellegrin. The great painting and gestural force of Emilio Vedova have been always closely associated with action and based around a limited chromatic range. From the

Ca' Pesaro is the majestic building designed in the Baroque era by Baldassarre Longhena for one of the wealthiest families of the time.

end of the seventies, using new technology, Fabrizio Plessi created an expressive language centered around a tight relationship between video sequencing and objects.

From the late eighties until the present, Maurizio Pellegrin has created cultured and refined works that are greatly influenced by eastern tradition. They range from paintings to installations, film, sculptures and photographs.

The Venice Biennale, having expanded with new and seductive exhibition spaces and via ambitious programs extended to all art fields, has sealed its own prominent international role in the promotion of culture. At the same time, Venice can count on other public and private institutions to support new generations of emerging artists who, despite the challenges, are preparing to leave an equally important mark.

SAINT MARK'S SQUARE

St. Mark's Square has always been the political center of Venice, and its exuberant display of symbols and meanings has stood witness to the history of the city itself. The magnificence of Saint Mark's Square is confirmed by the fact that it is the one true *piazza* (square) in Venice, and the only one to be called by that name: all other city squares are in fact referred to as *campi* (fields).

The government moved from Malamocco to Venice in the 9th century because its geographical position did not guarantee enough protection from enemy attacks. It was precisely in this period that the complex history of the Doge's Palace, the most important building of the Square, began. As the residence of the Doge – the most important figure of the State of St. Mark – the palace also functioned as a political, administrative and legislative center and represented the power of the Republic.

The Doge's apartments were richly decorated, with the family's coat of arms dominating the Shield Room. Following his election, each Doge outfitted his new residence with precious fixtures that belonged to him. Upon his death, they were removed by his family in order to vacate the rooms for his successor.

The Chief of State was elected through a complicated ballot system that lasted several days and aimed to prevent collusion or the formation of opposing factions. Lavish and lengthy inaugural ceremonies were conducted in the courtyard of the Doge's Palace, where the Doge himself –sumptuously dressed and surrounded by numerous symbolic objects – was crowned with the Doge's cap, a headdress bedecked with precious stones.

The Doge ruled for life, while the positions of other members and magistrates rotated periodically, since the Republic did not grant hereditary positions to patricians.

Originally, the Chief of State enjoyed unlimited power. Starting in the 11th century, however, his position changed radically. In addition to the privileges linked to his role, the Doge had to comply with a lengthy list of limitations: for example, he could not leave Venice without permission; he could not hold private audiences or open or send letters without the presence of a councilor; and he could not receive presents or make visits.

Moreover, the Doge could not abdicate without authorization, but he could be deposed; if he was a masterful politician, he was able to exercise great power, as in the case of the great Doges commemorated in history.

The Doge was viewed as the symbol of the Republic and was considered almost a sacred figure. In an emblematic portrait by Giovanni Bellini, the old Doge Leonardo

Facing page,
St. Mark's Basilica overlooks
the Piazza with five large
portals surmounted by
flamboyant arches.

Gentile Bellini,
Procession
in Saint Mark's Square, 1496.
Gallerie dell'Accademia.

Loredan is represented realistically by his somatic features, including the wrinkles that time had carved in his face, the aquiline nose, and the refined elegance: but he remains distant from the viewer. The aristocrat looks into the distance without revealing anything of his intimate character, displaying only the great dignity bestowed upon him by his position. Bellini did not paint the man, but the Doge. The members of the government were first and foremost representatives of the Republic, then men.

A good, solid political system effectively controlled and regulated all aspects of the citizen's life and of the acquired territories. The most important magistracies held their offices in the Doge's Palace. The Great Council was comprised of approximately two thousand members, all men older than 25 who belonged to the most aristocratic families of the city, and was the supreme governing body. The members of the Great Council met each Sunday in a great hall to discuss public affairs, presided over by the Doge.

Following pages,
night view of of the
Saint Mark's majestic façade.

Initially, the Senate consisted of sixty people elected by the Great Council, chosen from among those patricians who stood out for their acts of dedication to the Republic. It held executive power, dealing with administrative, economic and political tasks. On the other hand, the members of the Collegio debated proposals that were then presented to, and analyzed by, the Senate. They received visits from the most illustrious foreign subjects and from ambassadors in a hall that was superbly decorated in order to showcase the magnificence of Venice to the world. La Signoria consisted of the Doge, six councilors of the Doge (one for each of the city's six districts) and of three heads of the judicial magistracies. The Council of Ten, instead, consisted of the Doge, six councilors and ten members nominated by the Great Council who could not be re-elected. It had jurisdiction over political crimes, sex crimes including sodomy, other types of crimes, and over corporations and theaters. It also conducted anti-espionage activities.

The Porta della Carta,
refined example of Gothic
architecture, connects the
Doge's Palace to the
St. Mark's basilica.

The contemporary design aspect of the Doge's Palace is the result of a long and difficult process by which the building underwent a considerable number of restorations and expansions and succumbed to a number of tragic fires. It was built at the main harbor, the point where the Grand Canal flows into the lagoon, attracting a great number of admiring visitors who arrived by sea.

There remains nothing of the first buil-ding, but it probably had lateral towers of typical Byzantine origin and was construc-ted around a courtyard. Little remains also of the constructions of the 12th century, commissioned by the prodigiously wealthy Doge Sebastiano Ziani. The realization of the Palace into its contemporary state be-gan midway through the 14th century si-multaneously with the systematic restruc-turing of the surrounding area, which in-cluded new flooring and the construction

of bridges in stone. The imposing structure, the greatest example of late Gothic style, features a façade decorated with white and pink geometrical designs, traversed in the lower part by a double line of arches which were typical of the Venetian *palazzo-fondaco* (palace-warehouse), and adorned in the upper section with large pointed arch windows, crowned with white stone battlements.

The plastic decoration in the arcade and in the open gallery is of exceptional value. The symbolic subjects of the reliefs and the capitals conveyed important messages to a population that was largely illiterate and thus drew guidance for a morally precise conduct from these masterpieces. Reference to both social and civil life, e.g. professions, months, vices, virtues, were all clearly evident in the sculptured capitals that were easily comprehensible both by Venice's population, as well as by fo-

Detail of the Doge's Palace. The delicate decorative stonework is reminiscent of lacework, and belongs to late Gothic style.

Preceding pages,
view of the façade of
the Doge's Palace, symbol
of the Republic and its
political, administrative
and legislative centre.

The Giants' Staircase,
inside the Doge's Palace,
served as a majestic access to
the Doge's private quarters.

reign visitors. The Palace was built around the courtyard, which demonstrates a harmonious stratification of different styles; the spectacular Scala dei Giganti (Giants' Staircase), designed by Jacopo Sansovino in the 16th century, led to the Doge's apartments.

Connected to the Palace through the Ponte dei Sospiri (Bridge of Sighs), the prisons, which were called Piombi (Leads), took their name from the material used to build the roof, which caused the oppressive heat characteristic of this building during the summer. Hence, the prison cells located on the first floor were called Pozzi (Wells) because of the darkness and humidity that permeated them. The prisons of the Doge's Palace have been for years the object of intense literature, including accounts of the adventurous escape of Giacomo Casanova, which describe the horrific living conditions of prisoners (which did not always reflect the reality depicted in other documents). In fact, Venice's penitentiary system was more magnanimous than that of other cities because it guaranteed detainees legal assistance by court-appointed lawyers. Prisoners were also given fresh bread and were sometimes permitted to go out during the day.

The Palace's internal area was destroyed twice by devastating fires that took place in quick succession in 1574 and 1577, destroying works of the major artists of the time (Giovanni Bellini, Carpaccio, Titian, Veronese and Tintoretto). To quickly restore the magnificence of the most important symbol of the maritime Republic, the authorities duly summoned Veronese and Tintoretto, the only two painters still living when the disaster struck, and teamed them with Francesco Bassano, Palma il Giovane and the Roman Francesco Zuccari. The design was carefully defined: the walls would display episodes of the history of the Serenissima, while the ceiling would show allegories of the virtues and victories

at sea and on land which contributed to Venice's rise as a great power, along with portraits of the city's most famous and valiant citizens. The *Triumph of Venice* by Veronese is an exemplary model of a work of art with political meaning. The painting is structured with fantastic architecture and an upward-looking perspective, with common people at a lower level and patricians above.

Everyone in the painting is gazing upward toward the city of Venice, which is emblazoned in glory, surrounded by virtues and crowned by angels. On the periphery, two twisted columns recall those of the temple of Salomon, and impart a divine aura to the scene.

The St. Mark's basilica, which at one time was the chapel of the Palace, is connected to the Doge's Palace through the Porta della Carta. It was therefore the church of the State, used for all public functions, from the Doge's election ceremony to the blessing of soldiers going off to war. Above all, it was where St. Mark's body was preserved, having arrived in Venice after several vicissitudes. It is narrated that in the 9th century, two merchants took shelter with their ship in the port of Alexandria of Egypt during a terrible storm.

There they ran into two monks who, fearing that the Muslims were trying to demolish the temple in which the mortal remains of the evangelist were preserved, decided to exchange the body with the one of another saint. The four therefore hid the sacred remains of St. Mark in a basket and covered it with pork in order to deter the Muslim customs officers.

A number of miracles that took place during the return voyage affirmed the authenticity of the remains. As a sign of liberation from the Byzantine Empire, St. Mark replaced the patron saint of the city at the time, St. Theodore, who was of Greek-oriental origin. The figure associated with the evangelist is the winged lion,

which soon became the symbol of Venice (frequently represented in an "amphibious" form, with two legs in the water and two on the ground), and as such, represented the *status* of the Republic. The arrival of St. Mark's mortal remains was accompanied by the commencement of the construction of the basilica, which was radically modified in the 11th century. A structure similar to the present one was accomplished only at the end of the 15th century, following a long succession of additions and modifications.

The layout of the church bears the Greek cross structure with the intersection and each arm surmounted by five large cupolas, which together create an organic spatial layout in which spaces are interconnected with a myriad colonnades and arcades. Five great portals appear within the façade. At the rear of the entrance arch are four majestic horses purloined from the hippodrome of Constantinople during the conquest of 1204. Probably dating from the 2nd century and of Greek-Roman origin, they became a vigorous symbol of the

Aerial view of the domes of St. Mark's basilica.

power of Venice. Napoleon also understood their emblematic value, to the point that in 1797, he had them transferred to Paris before returning them a few years later.

The basilica can be accessed through a shadowy entrance hall that softens the effect within the passage of a strong external light, changing it into the dim light that conveys an almost supernatural quality due to the walls' gold-based leaf decoration. The mosaic, whose surface covers almost 4,000 square meters, depicts stories from the Old and New Testament. The precious marble flooring from the 12th century, refined with geometrical designs, animals and volutes, is a masterpiece that takes its place in the classical decorative tradition of the Northern Adriatic.

In the 11th century, the appearance of the Square was very different from that of today. It covered an area that is half the current size and ended in a little canal over which rose the church of S. Geminiano, while the Piazzetta (which the long side of the Doge's Palace overlooks today and which extends as far as the basin of St. Mark's) was a dock that left the ancient Doge's Palace surrounded by water on all sides.

In the following century, the appearance of the Square started to resemble its current structure: the dock and the canal were filled in and the position of the church was substantially receded. In 1264, the area was paved with terracotta bricks in a herringbone pattern, while the pavement we see today dates back to the middle of the 18th century.

The Clock Tower was built in the late 15th century and was probably designed by Mauro Codussi, whose expertise in construction was well established. The construction was based on an exquisite knowledge of Renaissance features and classical sources.

Built as a majestic portal for the Mercerie

(one of the most important streets of the city) and in harmony with the Piazzetta, the two columns and the basin of St. Mark, the Clock Tower offered a spectacular view to those arriving by sea. The building clearly displays a sense of proportion, the mastership of the new techniques and the great inventive ability of Codussi. Above the arch, the observer's gaze is caught by the large enameled dial on which are displayed the hours, the phases of the moon, a sundial, and the signs of the zodiac. A small terrace protrudes farther up: on the day of the Ascension, the figures of the Magi are paraded here, bowing before the Virgin Mary. At the top of the Tower, stretching skywards, are the *Mori*: solid, bronze-plated masculine figures which to this day mark the passage of time by striking a hammer against a bell.

In the first half of the 16th century, major shifts in European politics – with the newly configured constitution of large national States – relegated Venice for the first time to a state of inferiority. To counter the situation of decline the government chose a robust image, that of Rome, which was an indisputable symbol of power. The restoration of St. Mark's Square, political symbol of Venice, was commissioned to Jacopo Sansovino immediately following his arrival from Rome. Sansovino began evacuating the areas used for activities incompatible with the style of the Square. Stalls of butchers, sausage vendors and cheese producers had multiplied in the area between the two columns of the Piazzetta or along the jetty. They attracted throngs of citizens and foreign merchants, sullying the appearance of the Square and filling it with unpleasant odors.

In 1535, Sansovino redesigned the Zecca (the Mint, which in the 18th century was still producing a sizable percentage of the global currency) rendering it with its great arches, a classical look that was expertly modernized with Istrian stone rustication, while masterfully addressing the distribution of internal spaces – even taking into consideration the risks associated with theft and fire from the foundries occupying the building. Funding for the construction of the Mint appears to have been raised from proceeds collected by Venice for conceding freedom to the slaves of Cyprus at a cost of 50 ducats each.

Soon after, Sansovino began the creation of one of the most demanding and prestigious works of his life: the Biblioteca Marciana (Saint Mark's Library) opposite Doge's Palace, which was to house the extraordinary bequest of manuscripts and books from Cardinal Bessarione. The building stands upon two lines of superimposed arches, starting with columns and decorations of classical origin, a style also given to the sculptures that are prominently situated on the balustrade. The architect's tribute to ancient language is perfectly harmonized with the surrounding area in a play of volumes and empty spaces, of light and shadow, in a city where surfaces vibrate from the water's reflection. During construction, a part of the building collapsed, causing the death of a number of workers at the site. Sansovino was arrested in his capacity as head of works, and it was only thanks to the intervention of powerful friends, such as the famous Titian and the well-read Pietro Aretino, that he was freed. The architect subsequently continued with the construction at his own expense but was unable to see his work accomplished by the time of his death in 1570. Vincenzo Scamozzi was then entrusted with the task of seeing it to completion.

Among Sansovino's creations in the Square are Loggetta del Campanile (the Bell Tower Vestibule), Scala d'Oro and Scala dei Giganti in the Doge's Palace, a number of restoration works in the basilica, and finally the church of S. Geminiano on the side opposite to that of the basilica (which was later razed to the ground by Napoleon at the beginning of the 19th century).

Another emblem of St. Mark's Square is undoubtedly the Campanile, which was constructed in the 9th century and subsequently underwent several renovations. The Campanile that we see today, completed in the early 20th century, is a replica of the original from the 16th century. The latter collapsed in 1902, without causing extensive damage to the surrounding area. For many centuries, it had been a reference point for the citizens who would usually meet in its shade to chat, discuss business and politics. It is also the highest building in the city and, as such, served the auxiliary function of lighthouse for seafarers, and as well as watchtower. Its bells punctuated the civil rhythms and each one, with its specific tone, referred to a particular function in the sphere of daily and political life.

The tolls of the *Marangona* bell marked the beginning and the end of the working day. They also announced the time for meetings to the members of the Major Council, who were encouraged to be punctual by the tolling of the *Trottiera* bell. Then there was the bell for the meeting of the Senate which rang at midday and another that signaled capital executions.

The Bell Tower also bore witness to a particular form of punishment: the *cheba*. This was a wooden cage in which those found guilty were encased and hoisted by means of a rope along the length of the Bell Tower ten meters off the ground. This form of punishment was reserved in great measure for men of the church. The prisoners were fed for months on bread and water – on top of the humiliation, they had to endure both the rigors of cold as well as the unbearable summer heat. Another terrible punishment took place in St. Mark's Square between the two columns at the end of the Piazzetta. Those found guilty of particularly serious crimes or crimes against the State were paraded through the city on a flatboat, naked from the waist down and, during the trip, they were tortured with scrap iron; then, after undergoing amputation of the right arm, they were dragged through the streets to the two columns where they were then decapitated. Their bodies were subsequently quartered and displayed in public. In ancient times, other imaginative punishments were practiced depending on the gravity of the crime but it is appropriate to highlight that the prisoners in Venice were often treated more respectfully than elsewhere, and that torture was widely practiced, at least until the beginning of the 18th century.

The Square is surrounded by arcaded buildings: during the time of the Republic, these were the residences of the nine Procurators of San Marco. The Procurator's office was assigned to patricians who had demonstrated great service to the Republic.

The Procuratie Vecchie, rising to the right of the basilica, consists of a double open arcade, marked by a Venetian-Byzantine style cadenced by typical Renaissance-like classicism. On the opposite side are found the Procuratie Nuove, the construction of which was commenced by Vincenzo Scamozzi at the end of the 16th century and completed by Baldassarre Longhena in the following century. The classically inspired style of the two architects is in harmony with that of the Biblioteca Marciana, of which the Procuratie seemed to have been a natural extension. After having served the aims of those representatives of the Napoleonic government and becoming the Royal Palace, the majestic building of the Procuratie Nuove now houses museums and public offices while the Procuratie Vecchie are privately owned.

St. Mark's Square, so laden with meaning and symbolism, was also the perfect setting for town ceremonies and festivities that marked the life of the Republic. Codi-fied with a rigid hierarchy and by strict protocol, these rituals were enduring, almost timeless, and brought a sense of continuity and security to the population.

The most important and elaborate procession was the one taking place on the occasion of the Doge's election. Following the religious ceremony in St. Mark's basilica, before crossing the threshold of the Doge's Palace, the Doge paraded through the Square, where joyful throngs of people greeted him as he threw coins into the crowd. There were also many recurrent celebrations, such as that of the 25th of April, Saint Mark's Festivity, in which participated representatives of all social classes. Another joyous ceremony was that of Giovedì Grasso (Fat Thursday) which marked the closure of Carnival, with jugglers, acrobats, bull fighting and fireworks. An interesting iconographic account of this kind of display is the painting by Gentile Bellini of the *Procession in St. Mark's Square* of 1496. Always in the Square, impressive events were organized to welcome important visiting figures or to celebrate the victories of the Venetian navy and army. In their diaries, foreign visitors described extraordinary parties with music, balls, merry entertainment, and elegantly dressed, beautiful women; such worldly chronicles of a magnificent city, contributed to creating the legend of Venice.

On 12th May 1797, the enemy marched on Venice, and Napoleon's French soldiers eventually paraded triumphantly through St. Mark's Square. Having taken office, the emperor introduced radical administrative and urban measures, showing from the outset his wish to be present in St. Mark's Square, to demonstrate the power of the new government and to affirm the defeat of Venice, also called the *Dominante*. To this end, he transformed the Procuratie Nuove into the Royal Palace. He also demolished the ancient battlemented building which housed Venice's granaries on

the jetty, so as to gain an unobstructed view over the lagoon. Where what had been one of the symbols of wealth of the city are now flowering the Giardinetti Reali (the Royal Gardens). In 1807, the buildings which enclosed the Square opposite the St. Mark's basilica were razed to the ground, namely the Sansovinianan church of S. Geminiano and a part of the Procuratie Vecchie. The Ala Napoleonica (Napoleonic Wing) was later erected in that area, while the internal rooms, masterpieces of neoclassical art, are now the premises of the Museo Correr.

For centuries the anteroom of the Biblioteca Marciana hosted the incomparable Grimani collection, which gave life to one of the world's first museums.

GRAND CANAL

As with many large European cities, Venice sprang up on the banks of a flowing body of water. This was not a river but a canal of unusual size named the Grand Canal. The Grand Canal crosses the city in an 'S' shape and divides it into two parts, *de citra* and *de ultra*. With an average width of forty meters, it winds its way for forty kilometers from Piazzale Roma to the basin of Saint Mark. At this last point it is laterally bound by an outcrop of land on which the first customs house was built, the Dogana da Mar. It was here that goods coming from the sea were examined and taxed. The customs building, whose shape is patterned on the triangular form of the lip of land on which it was built, is well-known for the large golden sphere that sits atop the structure, visible to all seafarers from the mouths of the port, and representing the earth held by Atlas.

It was precisely on the banks of the Grand Canal, in the vicinity of a cove, that the first inhabitants of Venice settled. This place was named Rialto, and it soon became the most important Mediterranean trading pole. Merchant ships from all over the world sailed the waters of the lagoon to reach the mouth of the Grand Canal. Once at Rialto, they loaded and unloaded all types of goods, from produce to spices, from precious cloth to metals. The roads around Rialto teemed with traders and business agents of all nationalities, dressed in the most exotic fashions, and the air buzzed with the sound of a multitude of languages: Flemish, Greek, Turkish, German and Hebrew. This colorful crowd gathered for the common interest of doing business.

In the vibrant and bustling area of Rialto, money exchanged hands as bargains and retail sales were conducted, but all of this activity was strictly monitored by the government. All market activity was regulated by the state, which collected profits through taxes levied on every transaction. The authorities ensured that all transactions were executed in accordance to legislation via the many administrative offices in that area. Checks were carried out in different forms. For example, a public set of scales was erected at the access points of the Rialto Bridge to avoid smuggling. Anyone caught selling food that was no longer fresh, or found guilty of defrauding, was punished by incarceration. Workers, however, still enjoyed a relative form of protection from the authorities; in the case of fishmongers, for example, the fish was sold by old fisherman who were no longer able to go to sea, so as to guarantee them a form of pension. The

Facing page,
Punta della Dogana,
which was once
the place where
goods were inspected, is
famous for its great golden
globe, that is visible
to all seafarers.

For centuries, the Rialto Bridge, designed by Antonio da Ponte with two rows of shops, was the only bridge over the Grand Canal

central bakery for the production of bread was located in Rialto, with twenty five shops situated in the vicinity of the courts. The courts were responsible for monitoring prices and the quality of the wheat used for bread making. The production and sale of this staple foodstuff were regulated by strict laws. The bread could be white or whole meal or biscuit bread, but if the established requirements were not being adhered to, the goods were torn to pieces and thrown onto the steps of the Rialto Bridge.

The market was located nearby, where stalls were generally grouped according to the goods being sold. Shops were often very small outlets, as the rent – which was collected by the state – was very high. Some faced the crowded area in front of the church of S. Giacometto, the ancient Rialto church, where residents and foreign merchants kept up to date with the news and political developments.

The news of the day – from civil affairs to domestic and foreign politics – was announced at a location known as *pietra del bando*, which is still visible today.

It was in the Rialto area that the first residential blocks were built on the Grand Canal. These functioned as both houses and businesses, and were generally owned by members of the aristocracy. The buildings, which overlooked the water, were characterized on the lower level by a

loggia, a system of open arches that allowed for the loading and unloading of merchandise. The entrance hall to the ground floor served as a warehouse, while the small mezzanines were used as offices. The accommodations for the owners were situated on the main floor. Among the oldest examples of this residential design are Palazzo Cavalli and Palazzo Franchetti, both of which are now publicly owned.

The Rialto area also featured other kinds of buildings that were constructed around a courtyard. These were called *fondaci*, a name originating from the Arab *fonduq*, i.e. places where foreigners could conduct business. In Venice, fo-

reign merchants could trade, store their goods, and sleep in *fondaci*. These buildings were rented by the city to foreign communities, such as those from Milan, Lucca or Armenia.

Two examples still remain on the Grand Canal: Fondaco dei Turchi (the Turkish Warehouse), heavily altered in the 18th century and now housing the Museum of Natural History, and directly next to the Rialto; and Fondaco dei Tedeschi (the German Warehouse) now the central offices of the Post Office. This 15th century building was re-constructed after a fire destroyed the original one built in the 13th century. The latter was one of the most important and richest warehouses in

The Fondaco dei Tedeschi was the area where the German citizens carried out business and stored goods.

Facing page,
the Ca' d'Oro, once coated
with gold leaf and precious
marble, is a marvel of
domestic Gothic architecture.

Following pages,
the Grand Canal can be
admired from the refined mul-
ti-lancet windows of
the Ca' d'Oro, which are
a charming example of
Venice's late Gothic style.

the city, and all types of goods were stored there: carpets, jewels, cloths and metals. On the upper floors were the meeting rooms for foreign traders, and their accommodations.

The fire damage to the original building was such a devastating loss for German and Venetian trade that the Republic decided to build a new one. The Venetians assumed the cost, planning to recover it through rental fees. Today's building is of exceptional dimensions and is built around an inner courtyard surrounded by arches that create an almost metaphysical ambiance. The great Giorgione and his best student, Titian, were summoned in 1507 to create the frescoed decoration of the façade. A few pieces that have survived the battering of the elements and the lagoon's salty air are preserved in the Museum of Ca' d'Oro and in their uniqueness, represent exceptional testimony of fresco decoration on the Grand Canal. During those years, it was customary for the upper classes to decorate their homes with large, colorful frescoes depicting a wide range of themes, which varied according to the personality and requirements of the patron. Those who traveled by boat along the Grand Canal must have enjoyed a marvelous view of Venice in all its opulence and sophistication.

The entire marketplace area was also destroyed in 1514 by a terrible fire that devastated the premises in a matter of hours, fueled by the strong winter winds. The disastrous loss occurred at a particularly difficult time, following the taxing war against the League of Cambrai. The immediate reconstruction of the market area was of critical importance as it represented an essential source of income for the city. Furthermore, the citizens and the rest of the world needed to be shown that Venice was always able to recover from

setbacks and could count on endless resources. Antonio Scarpagnino, summoned to redesign the area, developed a more functional plan with wider, more passable roads and an improved layout of shops and offices.

For one thousand years, the Grand Canal could be crossed only on one bridge, located in the Rialto area. Originally it was probably just a boat bridge. A suitable wooden bridge was subsequently built; unfortunately the bridge collapsed halfway through the 15th century due to the weight of the crowd standing on it to attend the prestigious procession held on the occasion of the wedding of the Marquis of Ferrara. Later, another wooden bridge was built that supported two rows of shops. The central part, formed by a drawbridge, allowed ships to pass through. Vittore Carpaccio provided an accurate description of this latter construction at the end of the 15th century in his painting *The Miracle of the True Cross*. After a series of other accidents, the government finally decided to build a bridge made of stone.

As such, a competition was announced dictating that, among other requirements, the construction had to include shops and be high enough to allow the *Bucintoro*, the Doge's golden vessel, to pass under it. Great architects took part in this competition such as Sansovino, Michelangelo, Scamozzi and Palladio (whose majestic project, imbued with classical elegance, is represented in a painting by Canaletto). Finally, in 1588, the construction of the most important bridge in Venice was awarded to Antonio Da Ponte, who submitted a rather traditional project which was selected for execution.

The new Rialto Bridge remained the only one on the Grand Canal for many centuries until Ponte degli Scalzi and Ponte

dell'Accademia were built in the 19th century.

Though both were initially realized in cast iron, they were later reconstructed in the first half of the 20th century, the former from stone, and the latter from wood. Since then, the stretch of canal in front of Gallerie dell'Accademia is still crossed by Ponte dell'Accademia, which is periodically restored. The fourth bridge, called Ponte della Costituzione, connects the railway station to Piazzale Roma, the only area of Venice that is open to the circulation of motor vehicles. The project (completed in 2008 not without controversy) was designed by the Spanish architect Santiago Calatrava. This sleek bridge constitutes the most important piece of architectural work carried out in recent years. To date, Venice has remained rather resistant to the contemporary architectural spirit, as shown for example by the missed opportunities for the realization of projects by Frank Lloyd Wright and Le Corbusier.

Until the 14th century, various construction sites, workshops, dry docks with warehouses, equipment and collections of various materials could be found on the banks of the Grand Canal, giving a sense of unfinished disorder. At the time, people were generally unconcerned with appearances, hence it was hardly for aesthetic reasons that a law established that these activities had to be moved along the edges of the lagoon. This transfer took place because Venetians understood that the dumping of waste products into the Grand Canal risked compromising its navigability. The canal was used by all sorts of vessels, from small, light ones to 200 ton ships, all of which represented an essential resource for business. There were some exceptions, however, as demonstrated in an early 18th century painting by Canaletto in which a stone yard appears on the Grand Canal in front of the current Gallerie dell'Accademia. Among the traditional vessels that habitually traverse the Grand Canal, such as the *Caorlina*, the *Mascareta*, the *Sandolo* or the *Pupparin*, the most famous, undoubtedly, is the gondola. Already in use in the 11th century, the gondola over time experienced a gradual evolution, driven by a process of adaptation to the different needs of man and to the changes of the lagoon. It is a fast boat, with a flat bottom and with great capacity, characterized by a slightly asymmetrical shape which balances the weight of the *gondoliere*. Alone and using just one oar, the *gondoliere* can easily steer the vessel despite its considerable length, 11 meters. According to tradition, the iron combs of the prow represent the six areas into which Venice is divided, the stern-facing bar is the island of Giudecca and, the "S" shape represents the Grand Canal. In the 16th century the gondola soon became a status symbol for the affluent. It was often also used to ferry passengers from one bank to another. The trip was a comfortable alternative to a long walk, especially given that for centuries, only one bridge spanned the canal. Today, gondolas still ferry passengers back and forth.

The water doors of buildings on the Grand Canal are framed, as in the past, by smoothed tree trunks planted in the muddy soil, which have become a typical feature of the Venetian landscape. Often the poles are decorated at the top with pine cones and painted with colored spirals bearing a coat of arms: in addition to their symbolic value, they also serve the practical function of defining spaces and providing a landing place for the boats.

As the main thoroughfare of the city, the Grand Canal also became a splendid theatre for many regattas. During festivals, weddings or illustrious visits, different types of boats traveled the canal ri-

The Fondaco dei Turchi still preserves its old porch on the ground floor which was originally used for loading and unloading goods

chly decorated by the patrician families or by confraternities that challenged each other in captivating speed races. At such times, the buildings along the banks were transformed into spectacular sets. The public was able to admire the extraordinary spectacle of the building façades which seemed to sway along with the reflection of the water, rich in vibrant colors, and embellished with oriental marble and sophisticated Gothic decorations in Istrian stone. With the volumes and voids of the arched galleries and the chromatic variance of the plasterwork, the backdrop became even more multi-dimensional because it was customary, during special occasions, to display from the balconies, colorful carpets and tapestries.

To complete the picture, beautiful Venetian dames appeared at the windows:
known throughout the world for their
elegance, fancy hairstyles, jewelry, and
clothes of inestimable value, they boasted
the finest of local production.
The most famous regattas, besides those
that recurred annually, were those held
for Henry III King of France in 1574 and

for the Emperor Joseph II in 1775.
Regattas still take place every year in
which the traditional style of rowing while standing up is practiced. Some of the
most illustrious are the Regata Storica,
the Regata delle Marie and the Palio of
the Marine Republics in which, symboli-
cally, the ancient conflicts between Venice, Pisa, Genova and Amalfi are revived

*Following pages,
the banks of the Canal
Grande are beautifully
framed by almost
two hundred buildings
such as Ca' Giustinian
and Ca' Bernardo.*

PALACES

Venice's urban fabric has always had a rather heterogeneous character; as rich and poor citizens lived side by side in a relationship that was generally based on a sense of civility and exchange. This coexistence, which probably originated from the city's distinctive political-social structure, was also the result of an urban evolution that unfolded according to no particular urban development plan. Sumptuous residences and humble abodes faced each other over small courtyards or large *campi* (squares), imposing doors reared up beside little rickety doors, and lancet windows finely decorated in Istrian stone stood shoulder to shoulder with shabby looking windows.

It was the prerogative of all palaces to have their main entrance on the water. The door that opened onto the street, generally located in the rear of the building, was less important and was used principally by servants, and for the more menial tasks. In a world where waterways were used even more than roads, direct access to the canal was crucial for trade as well as for means of personal transport. The aristocratic families owned various types of boats for the transportation of goods necessary for their working lives, or for general daily needs or recreation. Almost all palaces were equipped with one or more gondolas, which were personalized with ornamental motifs, making them true jewels. The owners, comfortably seated, were transported by their *gondolieri* (oarsmen) along the canals, under the bridges and along the Grand Canal, for the purpose of visiting the residents of other palaces, running errands or attending the Sunday meetings of the Great Council.

The most prestigious palaces were concentrated along the Grand Canal, not just for status but for reasons of functionality, as it was the main thoroughfare of the city. These patrician residences were identified simply by the word *Ca'* – an abbreviation of the word 'casa' (house) – followed by the surname of the owners (as in Ca' Dario or Ca' Pesaro), occasionally accompanied by the name of the previous owner (as in Ca' Vendramin Calergi or Ca' Barbaro Curtis). When the same surname applied to different palaces, a distinctive feature of the building would be added to the name, as in the case of Ca' Contarini delle Figure (figures), Ca' Contarini del Bovolo (snail) or Ca' Corner della Regina (queen). The Doge's palace, the seat of the Governement, was the only palace in all of Venice worthy of the name "palace".

The palaces which rose from the waters of the lagoon, were famous worldwide for their architectural exactitude and the exquisiteness and splendor of their decorations, as testified by the admiring ac-

Facing page,
Alessandro Longhi,
La famiglia del procuratore
Luigi Pisani, 1758.
Gallerie dell'Accademia.

counts of traveling foreigners. The Venetian aristocracy, in fact, overlapped with the political class and had every reason to impress not only co-citizens but also ambassadors and foreigners who, for different reasons, descended upon the city. The accounts of visitors became a useful promotional tool and strengthened the strong image of Venice abroad.

The Venetian palace is a type of construction that is unique in the world. It has remained structurally unaltered for centuries, excepting the inevitable superficial modifications stemming from the trend of the period and the character of the owner. No examples of the original buildings remain, given that until the 10th century the materials used in construction were wood and hay, and brick and stone gradually started being used only at a later time. To understand the meaning of Venice's palace structure, one must bear in mind that these buildings were not only used for residential purposes, but also as the locus of trading activity for the family who lived there. Whilst in other Italian states and in European countries nobility's wealth came from land ownership, in Venice it was attributed to business and trade.

The oldest aristocratic dwellings date back to the 12th century, and were built in the typical Venetian-Byzantine style which characterized the general appearance of the young city. Palaces were bi-level structures to which other floors were added only later. The façade was characterized by a thorough symmetry: a loggia (which over the years disappeared) was located at water level, and on the floor above opened a multi-mullioned window, later flanked by two pairs of windows. On the ground floor was a large entrance hall, which could either take the shape of a "T" or an "L" or simply be rectangular, as during the Renaissance period when large side rooms were built. Goods were loaded and unloaded through the water door into the entrance hall, while the side rooms were used for warehousing or as offices.

Businessmen and merchants were received in the busy entrance hall as well as sophisticated guests who arrived with their private boats. Visitors were probably used to the mayhem caused by the traffic of workmen, staff and goods to be stored or packaged, ready for transportation. During that period, life was much more Spartan and needs were decisively fewer compared to those of subsequent centuries. Already by the Renaissance period, more attention was being paid to the appearance of the entrance halls: goods were being stored in large side rooms and walls were embellished with imposing coats of arms, weapons and armor along with the typical bench chests finely carved in wood.

At times, the ground floor was considered too damp and goods were instead stored in the loft space, but there was one incident where this solution caused difficulties. We have an account of a spectacular fire in 1523 that destroyed the magnificent palace on the Grand Canal of the procurator Giorgio Cornaro, who had just received several crates of sugar and cotton from Cyprus. The merchandise had been stored in the loft space, where brazier remained lit all night to dry the sugar. The residents were still asleep when the fire broke out, eventually gutting the building; some persons survived by lowering themselves from the window with a rope, but three people lost their lives under the thunderous collapse of the façade. The wealthy Cornaro family immediately set about calling Jacopo Sansovino to construct a building even more beautiful and imposing than the preceding one, which would take the name of Ca' Corner della Ca' Granda.

In the typical Venetian palace, the layout of the ground floor corresponded to that of the second floor, used for the owners' accommodation. The main reception hall,

called the *portego*, was located above the central axis of the entrance hall, flanked by the side rooms which served as living rooms, bedrooms or rooms for daily activities. Generally, access to the first floor was by an exterior staircase, which commenced at the courtyard located behind the building. Later on, staircases were moved to the entrance hall in order to avoid having to exit each time. The courtyard served the purpose of lighting indoor spaces, and different domestic chores were carried out in this area. In the middle of the courtyard was the well that supplied the house with drinking water. Beyond the courtyard at times grew a garden, usually quite small and surrounded by walls. In the palace the light entered from the front and from the back through large openings in the façade and seldom through the side windows. This was particularly true in the palaces on the Grand Canal, where construction was so crowded that buildings sprang up one attached to the other. The first examples of Venetian-Byzantine style buildings date back to the 13th century, characterized by a loggia in the style of the Roman villa. This was generally the case in

The dining room of the Palazzo Falier Canossa is decorated with mirrors, doors and wooden frames that completely line the walls.

Following pages, a fully ornamented room in the Palazzo Vendramin Calergi, currently used as a gaming room by the Casinò Municipale.

The ballroom of Palazzo Labia was decorated by Giandomenico Tiepolo with scenes from the story of Antony and Cleopatra

the ancient area of Rialto, examples being Ca' Da Mosto, Palazzo Donà della Madonetta, Palazzo Cavalli and Ca' Farsetti.

In the 14th century, Gothic elements began to infiltrate the Byzantine style, adapting to local taste and gradually becoming the architectural language typical of Venice, known as *gotico fiorito*. The palace façades were characterized by a symmetrical distribution of the openings, which were open loggias with trilobate arches at the centre, and by two windows on the side wings. With their decoration in Istrian stone, these windows recalled the intrica-

cy and sophistication of lacework. In the context of domestic architecture, the Gothic masterpiece is perhaps Ca' d'Oro, originally covered with gold leaf and precious marble. The design of the windows resembles the decoration of the Doge's Palace and boasts all the vanities of the owner.

Other significant examples of rigorous Gothic architecture are Ca' Foscari (now the seat of the University of Venice), Ca' Bernardo, Palazzo Giovannelli and the elegant Palazzo Soranzo Van Axel. Another outstanding piece of work is Palazzo

Pisani Moretta, whose sumptuous interiors depict the lifestyles of the 18th century with magnificent frescoes by Giambattista Tiepolo and Jacopo Guarana and grandiose Murano chandeliers.

Palazzo Barbaro became famous for the illustrious guests that stayed there (including, among others, Henry James and Monet). In addition to its precious art collection and the rare 18th century frescoes and stuccos.

Between the 15th and 16th centuries, the first balconies began to appear on building façades. Soon thereafter they became a typical Venetian architectural feature, achieving a sophisticated elegance because of the different stylistic forms of the balustrades.

Towards the end of the 15th century, a new style began to emerge within the urban landscape. One of the most interesting experiments of this transitional period is Ca' Dario, whose wonderful façade encrusted with polychrome marble (designed by Pietro Lombardo) served to revive local tradition in a new fashion. The Renaissance entered Venice with the architect Mauro Codussi, who designed the most ma-

The magnificent ballroom of Ca' Rezzonico bears witness to the ancient splendour of one of Venice's last great families.

gnificent example of civil architecture, Palazzo Vendramin Calergi (now housing the premises of the Casinò Municipale), which openly reflects the Tuscan prototype with the rhythmical regularity of its façade. The typical Renaissance features are recognizable here in the proportional harmony of the elements – the round arches, the pilasters and the classical capitals – whose decorative function was as important as the static-structural aspect. The imposing size and alternation of volumes and voids which characterized the high Roman Renaissance period is visible instead in Palazzo Grimani, the superb creation of Michele Sanmicheli. His work, with its realization of the thorough classical measurements, in many ways resembles the work of Sansovino in Ca' Corner della Ca' Granda or in Palazzo Dolfin.

With the growing popularity of Baroque, it was Baldassarre Longhena who dominated the Venetian landscape, creating large-scale private architectural works in which he managed to communicate an impression of majestic movement. This was achieved thanks to the airy volumes and *chiaroscuri* generated by the use of Istrian stone (an example is Ca' Pesaro, now the Galleria Internazionale d'Arte Moderna). In the 18th century, Massari built Palazzo Grassi and Antonio Visentini designed the neoclassical façade of Palazzo Smith Mangilli Valmarana for Joseph Smith, the famous art collector. No other architects left any lasting impression during this period. The surviving interiors of the patricians' residences are largely 18th century; only a few traces – fireplaces, portals and ceilings – of the Renaissance and earlier periods survive.

The layout of the space is evidence of how life was conducted in the palaces: work areas, the composition of the family, the dynamics between relatives, the receiving of guests, and the role of servants and their designated tasks.

The most important room of the palace was the *portego*, a vast reception space with soaring four – or five – meter high ceilings, up to six meters wide and twenty-five meters long. Traditionally, this room was furnished only along the walls, with chests, foldable chairs or uncomfortable benches. Tables were not used, and meals were taken on chests or on long boards supported by stands that could be moved rapidly by the servants as required. The family, for practical reasons, rarely used the *portego* because it was impossible to heat such a large room. More often than not, it was used on the occasion of important visits or special events during which guests could appreciate the magnificent taste of the owner and admire the coat of arms engraved or painted on furniture and on the walls.

Family members occupied the side rooms, where large fireplaces created a comfortable setting. In these chambers, the bed was often covered with a canopy, whose precious fabrics retained the heat. These large rooms were richly decorated because they were also used to receive guests, a custom that today seems odd but in former times was widespread. The notion of privacy was very different from today's, as evidenced by the use of intercommunicating rooms. Furthermore, a number of nuclear families often co-habited, linked by a common male ascendancy; the sons often remained in the paternal house to which they brought their wives when they eventually married.

During the day, servants were present in the house, but in the evening they generally retired to their loft rooms, identifiable from the outside by small square windows.

In the old palaces, cupboards were unheard of and clothes were kept in chests which were true works of art. These often entered the house as dowries of the bride, as a symbol of opulence of the family that

presented them. Finely engraved and gilded, they were often decorated with painted stories and served many functions. In any given day these chests could be used as chairs, tables and steps, among other purposes.

The walls of the rooms were covered with precious fabrics, and later by the typical *cuori d'oro,* decorated leather linings which conferred to the environment a warm and comfortable ambience. At the end of the 17th century, a new trend rapidly took root, replacing preceding styles and gaining in popularity throughout the

following century. This consisted of lining; the walls of the *portego*, of small living rooms and of large bedrooms with rich decorations in stucco, set upon delicate pastel colored plaster. The reception rooms were enriched with frescos or canvases depicting important events in the history of the family; weddings, military victories, and investitures were often celebrated with allegorical compositions by famous artists of the time. The most intimate spaces contained smaller paintings such as portraits, fanciful *capricci* and bucolic landscapes.

*Palazzo Contarini delle
Figure displays the
harmonious coexistence
of contemporary furniture
with elements
of classical style.*

*Following pages,
the ballroom in Palazzo
Zenobio is a masterpiece
of late Baroque decoration,
rich in stuccoes
and trompe-l'œil.*

The furniture, which had acquired an affluent appearance, was often arranged along the walls and included exquisitely carved *trumeau*, chairs, armchairs, sofas, *consoles,* and *guéridon* with gilt designs along with floral motifs, volute and *rocaille*. As the terms used to describe the different types of furniture testify, French manner was very popular in furnishings, just as it was in fashion. In Venice, a predilection for varnished furniture survived for a long time because of its vibrant colors, which brought the rooms to life along with the magnificent Murano glass chandeliers and grandiose mirrors. An item that was always present was the harpsichord, an instrument played by the ladies of the house to entertain the guests during their frequent visits.

The distinctive floor of houses on the lagoon's islands was the *terrazzo alla veneziana*, still built today with the same technique above flexible wooden flooring. It was very light and elastic in order to support the continuous shifting, oscillation and adjustments of these buildings, which are built on soft soil. The actual floor, made from a mortar, was often brick-red in color studded with fragments of different material such as colored marble, glass and mother-of-pearl, was laid over a preparation of lime compound that was spread over the wood.

The standard of living of many Venetian noble families was extremely high. In order to impress neighbors or visiting foreigners with their wealth, patricians often reached the point of exaggeration, as demonstrated by the written accounts of a number of witnesses. They speak of a banquet held at Palazzo Pisani at San Beneto for Gustavo III of Sweden a few years before the fall of the Republic in 1784. A sumptuous dinner for eight hundred people was prepared with a hundred and sixty bombardiers as guards of honor. The guests, whose meals were served from platters made of solid gold, were presented with an endless display of delicious courses, served by hundreds of servants against a backdrop of tapestry-lined walls of velvet green and gold cloth, adorned especially for the occasion.

The Labias, an extremely affluent family of Spanish origin, were also famous for their luxurious parties. Some accounts claim that at the end of the lavish banquets, guests could throw solid gold plates, cutlery and glasses out of a window as proof of the wealth of their hosts (but the accounts also report that servants waited under the windows with nets to recover the precious items).

In order to ensure continuity in the prestige of the lineage, patrician families placed special emphasis on preserving the ancestral capital, and the interests of the individual took second place to that of the family. To preserve the family's heritage, only a few brothers were permitted to marry, and many girls entered a convent irrespective of their vocation. Marriages were the result of long diplomatic negotiations between families, with the future bride represented by the father or by a male member of her family and the promised bride and groom bowing to the wishes of their parents for the sake of the dynasty's convenience.

Marriage was a contract of great value and demanded suitable celebrations. Festivities lasted for several days in alternating banquets, ceremonies, balls and rituals for which no expense was spared. The townhouses of the future couple were decorated externally with rugs and tapestries, creating a joyful and festive polychrome effect which also involved the city. On the day of the wedding, the girls, who had always lead a retired life, were displayed as symbols of wealth for their families. The bride appeared in public dressed in white, her long hair loose around her shoulders, wearing magnificent jewels and, as dicta-

ted by tradition, a pearl necklace. The dowry was a fundamental contractual element in the union of the couple. It consisted of cash, property and furniture and, naturally, it included a *trousseau* of jewels, clothes and embroidered linen, in addition to the luxurious chests in which these items were stored.

The wedding could also be a prestigious occasion for restorations and important decorative tasks in the house of the groom, often with extraordinary results, as in the case of the ceilings painted by Giambattista Tiepolo at Ca' Rezzonico for the marriage of Ludovico Rezzonico to Faustina Savorgnan, or at Palazzo Manin for the marriage of Ludovico Manin to Elisabetta Grimani.

The fall of the Republic led to the ruin of many families and the consequent dispersal of a vast amount of assets. However, many palaces remain today, and their wealth has fortunately been preserved, further enhancing the great treasure of Venice.

Palazzo Dandolo, now the Hotel Danieli, is characterized by its ramped staircase which extends up the entire height of the foyer.

Following pages, the hall at Palazzo Pisani Moretta is splendidly decorated with eighteenth century elements.

PLACES OF WORSHIP

Religion was one of the pillars of Venice. In fact, in Venice, as in the rest of Europe, from Medieval times to the end of the Modern Era, the Christian experience influenced all aspects of personal and social life. Religion informed the spiritual, moral and everyday life of the city's inhabitants, marking the rhythm of their days through mass, bells and ceremonies. The various churches – one in each *campo* (square) – were the spiritual centres of the community, where the most important moments of the citizens' lives of each social class were celebrated: births, weddings and deaths.

Each parish normally consisted of about a thousand believers. Wealthier members took to realizing duties linked to the church, occupying themselves with renovations, additions and the commissioning of altarpieces. Parish churches were generally small, and in the 16th century about sixty of them were distributed across in the city.

Beyond the spiritual sphere, mass constituted an important moment in the social life of the community because it allowed the population to meet. After exiting the church, women chatted and men went to drink a glass of wine at the tavern. For young ladies of the upper class, whose lives unfolded within domestic walls, usually with a husband chosen by their family, mass was an opportunity to walk around freely in the open.

The churches soon became precious treasure caskets where today we can still find numerous paintings by great masters, sculptures, marble decorations, magnificent collections of silver and fabrics, wooden carvings and inlaid stones. The collection of these riches took place over the course of centuries, thanks to the charitable actions of the faithful: from the legacies of illustrious characters who, through their generosity, hoped to reach Heaven, to offerings by men and women who, in exchange, asked for a certain number of masses for the salvation of their own souls or that of a deceased relative.

The history of the Venetian places of worship developed alongside that of the city, starting from its initial relation with the Byzantine world. In all probability, by virtue of the traditional close contact with the Eastern Roman Empire, Venice had a different relationship with the Church of Rome compared to the other Italian states, which allowed it to maintain a certain degree of autonomy. This independence did not however prevent serious tensions from arising. At the beginning of the 17th century, the Pope was obliged to issue an interdict against the Republic, but the Senate stopped its publication within its own territories, nullifying in this way the power of

Facing page,
Titian, Assumption of the Virgin, *1516-18.*
Santa Maria Gloriosa dei Frari. Detail

The small church of San Giacometto still bears its old bell gable, clock and Gothic portico.

the Pope himself. Only after one year of skilful diplomatic negotiation was it possible to find a resolution to the clash. Venice was also excommunicated on a number of occasions, due to its trading and cultural links with the "infidel" Turks, though these measures did not attain the results hoped for by the Pope.

The independence of Venice was eloquently symbolized in St. Mark's basilica, the city's most important and splendid church, which however was not the cathedral but the chapel of the Doge's Palace, and was thus positioned within a secular rather than religious sphere. Appointment to the highest ecclesiastic positions fell to the Republic, while citizens elected their parish priest. This autonomy within Venice, even in the choice of its spiritual guides, precluded any kind of interference from the Church of Rome, which was merely notified of the appointments.

Nothing remains of the first temples, built with wood and topped by a roof made of straw, such as the great church of S. Salvador. Generally, churches were built in places where sacred buildings had previously stood, from which their name was then taken. The oldest churches in the lagoon are found today on the islands of Torcello and Murano, while the oldest parish church in the city, S. Giacometto, is in Rialto. The temple was rebuilt in the 11th century and was later miraculously saved from a fire that devastated the entire area in 1514. The citizens also loved it due to its legendary construction, which took place in 421, the same year in which, according to tradition, Venice was founded. The Greek cross plan, with its central cupola sustained by columns, recaptures the ancient Byzantine structural layout. The internal area is relatively small because the function of the parish church was to welcome only the residents of the area, even though that particular area was frequented also by traders and Catholic merchants who met to do business in the crowded square op-

posite the church. The façade, with its big 15th century clock, has a unique appearance, different from that of other churches of the same period, such as S. Zan Degolà or S. Nicolò dei Mendicoli.

Around the 13th century, a new model for places of worship appeared in Venice: the majestic temples of the Mendicant orders. The State favored their establishment because they represented a weapon with

which to combat the risk of heresy that was already widespread throughout Europe. Venice, along with other cities of the time, also designated a number of areas beyond the residential perimeter for these followers: in the first half of the 13th century, the Doge conceded to the Dominicans and Franciscans two areas of uninhabited marshlands on which, following extensive work, the grandiose churches of SS Gio-

The church of San Giacometto
with its ancient clock
is at the center of
the busy Rialto market area.

The ancient church of San Nicolò dei Mendicoli is a fine example of Venetian-Byzantine architecture.

Facing page, Santa Maria Gloriosa dei Frari, a grand example of Gothic style, is characterized by its typical tripartite brick façade.

vanni and Paolo and S. Maria Gloriosa dei Frari were, respectively, constructed. As majestic examples of the Gothic style, these temples introduced the constructive and stylistic tradition of the north, yet with different accents: the interiors are less harsh than those of the churches of France or England, and the spaces are more open, with lower ceilings and a theme of massive cylindrical columns. The common feature is the Latin cross layout, typical of convent churches, with their large naves designed to receive and reach a considerable number of followers and little chapels for the prayer times of nuns. These churches are characterized by visible brickwork, a treble façade refined only by a central rose window, pinnacles and decorations in white Istrian stone similar to other small temples, such as Madonna dell'Orto, S. Gregorio and S. Alvise.

The Gothic style, as already stated, defined Venice for a considerable length of time, and was substituted by the Renaissance style relatively late when compared to

Florence. The first work created in the Renaissance style was the church of S. Michele in Isola, designed by Mauro Codussi in 1469. The temple is situated on the waters of the lagoon with a façade in treble light-rusticated pilasters, entirely covered by white Istrian stone – a completely innovative appearance in the contemporary context, combined with the purity and temperance derived from the limited number of architectonical elements.

Codussi used some of the features, such as the small central lunette and the lateral quadrants, in the important church of S. Zaccaria. The latter became famous not only for its collection of artistic masterpieces and the exquisitely created façade, but also for the annual visit of the Doge. The head of state visited it publicly with his entourage as a sign of gratitude to the rich nuns of the adjacent convent who had given a large area of land to facilitate the widening of St. Mark's Square.

Codussi was also involved in the project for the church of S. Maria Formosa, a mo-

The church of San Pietro di Castello, with its classical façade, was originally the seat of the Bishop of Venice.

re complex and elaborate task, considered unique because of its remarkable organization of internal space, which, due to an optical illusion, seems to the visitor to be almost without limits. The architect designed arches, columns and chapels so that participants in the Doge's procession, which took place every year and moved at a slow pace, would enjoy the constantly changing perspectives.

Legend narrates that the procession was inspired by an event that took place in the 10th century. It all began during a ceremony in the church of S. Piero di Castello where twelve virtuous girls were receiving a dowry from the Government that would allow them to marry.

A gang of violent pirates interrupted the solemnity of the moment by abducting the girls, along with a number of valuables, and killing some people in the process. A group of carpenters of the parish of S. Maria Formosa followed the aggressors by sea to Caorle and, after defeating the pirates, returned with the girls and the booty. As a sign of gratitude, the Doge committed to visiting their church each year on a set date.

At the end of the 15th century, Pietro Lombardo began to construct the small and precious church of S. Maria dei Miracoli, which took its name from a votive image of the Madonna, known for having produced a considerable number of miracles, all recorded and described in minute detail. The many donations from private individuals, encouraged by the prodigious image, allowed the construction of this exquisite jewel, rendered unique due to its polychrome marble encrusted walls and by the refinement of the details. However, from an architectonical point of view, despite its

charm, S. Maria dei Miracoli is a world away from the formal purity of the Renaissance works of Codussi.

In the second half of the 16th century, after Jacopo Sansovino had realized his first projects for S. Salvador and S. Francesco della Vigna as a result of in depth studies on proportions and modular dimensions, Andrea Palladio began to operate in Venice. The famous architect planned three extraordinary temples that look out onto the city from the islands of S. Giorgio Maggiore and Giudecca. The most famous and charming of these is the church of the Re-

Following pages, left, the church of San Giorgio dei Greci and, right, the Baroque church of Santa Maria della Misericordia, part of the very ancient monumental complex of the Misericordia.

dentore, built following the request of the Senate as a vow in order to free inhabitants from the terrible plague of 1576 that killed around 50,000 people (including the great master Titian). It was created therefore as a votive temple and point of arrival for an important procession that took place every third Sunday of July, setting off from the Fondamenta delle Zattere over a long bridge of boats across the Canale della Giudecca. From this point on, the ceremony and the related feast of the Redentore engaged the entire population. In modern times, the celebration of the recurrent event takes place on the water facing the church on various boats decorated with lamps and vivid colors. On their boats, Venetians enjoy a magnificent display of fireworks, and then eat typical dishes, drink and dance until late into the night.

Palladian churches conveyed a sense of stern magnificence through their facades inspired by the classical temples, their interiors characterized by wide spaces of white plaster and Istrian stone, bathed in an intense light.

Without a doubt, the most important sacred construction of the Baroque era was the church of S. Maria della Salute, the imposing work of Baldassarre Longhena erected in the first half of the 17th century as a solemn vow to the Madonna so that Venice would be saved from another terrible plague. The temple, commissioned by the State, was meant to be a symbol of the rebirth of the city. Situated at the entrance to the Grand Canal, shining with its luminous Istrian stone, it rises majestically on an octagonal plan and is surmounted by a spacious central cupola supported by a series of twin volutes which, despite the Baroque flavor, reinforce its severity.

Like S. Maria Formosa, the plan in this case was also derived from ritual requirements. Architecture therefore became an integral part of the ceremonial: upon entering the premises, the faithful participating

in the procession had to have an all round vision of the place thanks to the circular plan; as they moved forward, the perspective changed continuously due to the flow of the eight chapels in a spoke-like formation radiating from the centre.

To imbue the building with an even more enhanced sacred quality, on the opposite bank, at water level, were sculpted two cherubs, which, as tradition dictates, brought the church from the sky to the earth. The 21st of November is the holiday of the Madonna della Salute, still a greatly heartfelt event for Venetians. For centuries, every year a votive bridge of ships is built across the Grand Canal, allowing the faithful from all parts of the city to access the church in order to pray, offer a white candle to the Madonna and ask for good health for themselves and their loved ones. Of the churches built in subsequent periods, the most noteworthy ones are those of S. Stae, S. Maria del Giglio and the great church dei Gesuiti, characterized by a façade brought to life by voluminous statues, niches and decorations.

In the 18th century, the language became more sober, as in the churches of the Tolentini or S. Simeon Piccolo, where the pronao, interpreting Palladian classicism, suggests the stylistic features of the Greek-Roman temple.

Catholicism was not the only religion practiced in the lagoon. As an international city with a long history of openness, Venice tolerated – even if with some difficulty – , the presence of other cultures, for example that of Greek-Orthodoxy. The Greek community, having expanded to 4,000 members with the growing emigration from the Peloponnese due to the Turkish threat, became one of the largest foreign presences. Venice always greeted the Greeks favorably due to their culture and great availability of resources, allowing them to found a school, the Greek-Orthodox confraternity, but was more reluctant to al-

low them to build a place of worship. In the 16th century, after innumerable attempts, and thanks to the support of the Hellenic soldiers in the war of Venice against the Turkish army, the Greeks succeeded in obtaining permission to purchase a piece of land in order to erect a temple dedicated to S. Giorgio. Externally, the church of S. Giorgio of the Greeks is similar to other Venetian churches of the time, yet it is uniquely orthodox inside. Its rich interior is adorned with a splendid iconostasis created by a skilful iconographer who had come from Crete precisely for its realization.

After the fall of the Republic, the Hellenic community encountered many difficulties due to massive confiscations effected by Napoleon, and many of its members left Venice. However, a small community of Greeks still lives around the church complex, today, a group that succeeded in maintaining its property and cultural heritage and that founded in 1948 the *Istituto*

The Schola Levantina, characterized by its wooden decorations by the school of Brustolon, is one of the five synagogues still remaining in the Ghetto.

This page, aerial view of the church of Santa Maria della Salute, glowing with its luminous Istrian stone stands monumentally on its octagonal plan.

Facing page, the church of Santa Maria della Salute, designed by Baldassarre Longhena, is the most important sacred building of the Baroque era.

Following pages, left, the church of San Moisè displays all the prominence of the Baroque style with its intensely sculpted exuberant façade. Right, the Madonna dei Miracoli is an exquisite jewel, whose uniqueness comes from its walls, encrusted in polychrome marble.

Ellenico di Studi Bizantini e Postbizantini (Hellenic Institute of Byzantine and post-Byzantine Studies).

Another great culture of the Mediterranean basin hosted by Venice was that of the Jews. The Jewish population lived, worked and practised its religion within the confines of the area allocated by the government, known as the Ghetto. Officially established by deliberation of the senate of 29th March 1516, this area had its spiritual heart in the synagogues, also called *scholae* similar to the Venetian confraternities. Nine of them were built, and the first three were very small and rather difficult to locate as they were situated on the top floors of inhabited buildings. The first Jews who arrived in Venice were Italians and Germans, and one of the oldest European synagogues, built in 1528, was German.

With the passing of time, the spaces assigned to the Jews were no longer adequate, which led to the encompassment of another area, the Ghetto Vecchio (Old Ghetto), where the richer Spanish and Levantine Jews were to settle.

Their synagogues were no longer hidden but became majestic temples that were later remodeled on the Baroque style, such as the Ponentina, rebuilt in the 17th century probably by the great architect Baldassarre Longhena. In 1633, with further extension, the Ghetto Novissimo (Very New Ghetto) was established where the Sephardic Jews settled. To this day, the Ghetto continues to host the Jewish community, tragically decimated by the Nazi deportations.

The spiritual centres are still the five surviving synagogues which take their names from the different branches of the community upon which they were founded, such as the Schola Tedesca, the Schola Italiana or the Schola Levantina.

Schools

In Venice there were three distinct social classes, each of which could work with the other and also practice the same profession; but outside of these spheres, it was very difficult for them to mix. The ruling class was made up of the nobility, which represented about 5% of the population and whose members were the only ones eligible to hold positions at a high political level. The other classes included citizens (also representing 5% of the population); and the rest of the population.

The patricians, the only holders of power in the 16th century, established the *Golden Book*, made up of the *Book of Births* and the *Book of Marriages*, a true civil registry of the aristocrats. A century later, at a time of hardship and in response to the need to raise revenue, the State opened the *Golden Book* to merchants, artisans and even foreigners, who could join the patrician class in exchange for large contributions.

Citizens were divided into two categories, those who were Venetian by birth and those who became citizens after a lengthy process of naturalization. Professionals, employees of the bureaucracy and merchants were generally citizens. Members of this class did not hold political power but could exert some influence through the *scuole* (schools), where the most illustrious citizens held important roles.

The third class consisted of the general population: artisans, small traders, workers and seamen. These people were not necessarily poor, just as the patricians were not necessarily rich. The general population gathered in the schools, which were associations of a devotional nature with the aim of mutual assistance, constituting both an important guarantee against poverty and playing a crucial role in protecting individuals and families in need. The economic foundation of these brotherhoods was based on a tax levied upon each member and on the testamentary bequests of wealthy brothers. The members of these schools were exceptionally united and helped each other in various ways: attending the funerals of their comrades in order to avoid a lonely death, caring for orphans and widows, organizing the dowry of destitute girls, attending to the sick and even building houses (upon which a symbol of the school is still visible today) for the homeless.

The sense of belonging generated by the schools contributed greatly to the development of a stable society. Unlike other major European cities, Venice in fact did not experience – except in ancient times – revolts or popular uprisings. The schools depended on the State, which simultaneously exercised a protective and monitoring role. Each had a patron saint, a statute and

Facing page,
Giovanni Mansueti,
The Miraculous Healing of
the Daugher of Benvegnudo
da San Polo, *c.1505.*
Gallerie dell'Accademia.

Bernardo Bellotto, The Rio dei Mendicanti and the Scuola di San Marco, 1740. Gallerie dell'Accademia.

Facing page, The scuola Grande di San Marco was located in this building, its façade covered with polychrome marble.

Following pages, view of the Scuola Grande di San Marco and of the church of SS Giovanni e Paolo.

its own symbols and emblems. In the 16th century more than two hundred such schools existed, enrolling about two hundred members to which were added six Scuole Grandi (Big Schools) with a maximum number of six hundred. The *Scuole Grandi* included individuals who had diverse occupations while the *Scuole Piccole* (Small Schools) could be purely devotional or corporate. The need for professional groups to congregate gave rise to a great number of trade schools, such as those for hairdressers, blacksmiths, fruit sellers, masons or wine merchants. Even foreigners, in order to overcome the lack of protection by the State and strengthen a national or religious identity, founded several schools, such as the Scuola degli Albanesi (Albanians), San Nicolò dei Greci (Greeks) and San Giorgio degli Schiavoni (Dalmatians). An interesting aspect of the *Scuole Piccole* was the presence of women who were otherwise marginalized in society: they were auxiliary members who could

elect their representatives, make decisions and enjoy a degree of influence within the institution.

The wealthier confraternities were able to afford premises of great artistic value (such as Scuola Grande di San Rocco, San Marco or San Giovanni Evangelista). The buildings that housed schools generally had the same layout: the room on the ground floor was typically divided into three sections by two colonnades and a staircase led to the upper level which consisted of a large room and a smaller space called *albergo*, designed for meetings and safeguarding the treasury.

Depending on their means, schools commissioned works of art, which could be simple altarpieces kept in a nearby church or valuable decorative cycles created for the school itself. The subjects of the paintings were generally religious but in some cases could also have interesting secular and local connotations. The wealthiest confraternities would commission major

works. For example, Scuola Grande di San Giovanni Evangelista commissioned the narration of the miracles made by the relic of the True Cross that was in its possession. This sacred fragment, jealously guarded throughout the whole year, was carried through the streets of the city during a particular ceremony. Members of the schools placed great importance on paintings as visual proof of their priceless treasures. At that time very few people were literate, so that imagery was the most direct way to indoctrinate people and increase the number of devotees.

In 1496, Gentile Bellini was appointed by Scuola Grande di San Giovanni Evangelista to paint the *Procession in St. Mark's Square*. In Venice, processions held great civic as well as religious value; they created continuity through rituals familiar to participants and spectators, and were carried out season after season, unchanged by time. In the painting by Gentile Bellini, the school's brothers are dressed in white; the procurators and senators of the Republic wear red gowns, and the patricians and the citizens wear black. The painting depicts Venice celebrating the feast of St. Mark (the 25th of April), patron saint of the city, during which a fragment of the True Cross was displayed. In the midst of the procession is a man in prayer. He is a merchant from Brescia who, having arrived in Venice for business, received the terrible news that his beloved son was in critical condition having hit his head. The next day, the man, aware of the powers of the True Cross, went to attend the ceremony, and when the famous relic passed in front of him, he knelt before it as a sign of devotion. When he returned home, he found his child miraculously healed.

The incident took place in St. Mark's Square, which is reproduced by Bellini in striking detail, providing an interesting visual document of the square at the end of the 15th century. Differences can be noticed if compared with today's St. Mark's Square such as the absence of the Clock Tower, the Ospizio Orseolo, where now are the Procuratie Nuove, and the old herringbone design paving replaced by the present one in the middle of the 18th century.

The square is populated by a number of people elegantly dressed in the fashion of the time: some young people in multicolored stockings, a group of Jews, a number of Turks wearing turbans, merchants and children. On the left women look out from the windows and a colorful range of carpets is displayed from balconies as a sign of celebration.

A more confusing scene is in the picture by Giovanni Mansueti, *Miracle of the Relic of the Holy Cross in Campo San Lio*, created again for Scuola Grande di San Giovanni Evangelista. The painting, hard to interpret, represents the funeral of a brother whose life had not been particularly virtuous. In addition to claiming no belief in the True Cross, the man had frequented taverns and places of ill repute. As was typical in such schools, his companions, invariably dressed in white, participated in the funeral procession by carrying the sacred fragment that refused to follow the coffin of the blasphemous character. On S. Lio bridge, the weight of the True Cross became so unbearable that the brothers were forced to lay it down and replace it with another relic.

Another story painted by Mansueti, takes place in an interior. It is the *Miraculous Healing of the Daughter of Benvegnudo of San Polo*. The artist here tells of a miracle that took place in 1414 when the daughter of a brother, who had been blind from birth, was healed. The little girl was three years old when her father touched her with the three candles that had been in contact with the True Cross. Mansueti painted the magnificent building where the event took place as a cross-cutting section, allowing

the viewer to easily observe the scene. On the left, on the first floor, runs a canal crossed by gondolas. Nearby are a number of men, young and old, and even a character with a turban and a cheetah on a leash. At the top, on the second floor to the right of the fireplace, sitting on the bed, is the healed child.

Vittore Carpaccio related another miracle of the True Cross in *The Healing of the Madman*. The event took place in the Patriarch of Grado's palace on the Grand Canal, and in the background one can see Rialto Bridge as it was in 1494, constructed in wood, with two rows of shops on the sides. The central part of the bridge could be lifted to allow the passage of ships. The brightly colored palaces have on their roofs a number of finely decorated chimneys, and in the distance are a number of *altane* (roof wooden terraces) with laundry hung out to dry, and beyond is a woman beating a carpet and several men in turbans, confirming the multiculturalism of the Rialto area, visited by merchants from all over the world. The main action takes place on the left where the Patriarch is seen raising the relic before the possessed man who fixes on it a glassy-eyed stare. The miracle is in progress, a dramatic moment made even more realistic by the fact that the scene takes place in a marginal position. The white

The Renaissance portal of the Scuola Grande di San Giovanni Evangelista is topped by an eagle, which is the symbol of this evangelist.

tunics of the brethren surround the scene, while all around life unfolds quietly, and it seems that few are aware of what is happening. Amongst the traffic on the Grand Canal is an unusual African gondolier, probably a slave, apparently well integrated into the life of Venice. Until the beginning of the 17th century, slavery was fairly common in Venice; the merchants collected slaves on the Dalmatian coast and in Russia, Mongolia, Turkey and Africa for resale in the public markets.

In 1504, Gentile Bellini was commissioned by Scuola Grande di San Marco to paint *St. Mark Preaching in Alexandria, Egypt,* but the artist died before the painting was completed. Thus, it was completed by his brother Giovanni Bellini, who had probably never been to Alexandria. For the realization of costumes and architectural details, Gentile drew free inspiration from one of his stays in Constantinople and from travel accounts. The layout of the painting is reminiscent of *Procession in St. Mark's Square,* where the characters in the foreground are in profile. The saint preaches from a small podium placed between the brothers and the Arabs, while in the background stands a great temple whose façade divided into three brings to mind, at the same time, the Scuola Grande di San Marco, the basilica di San Marco and the mosque of Hagia Sophia in Constantinople. Nearby there is also an obelisk engraved with hieroglyphics and several minarets. In the square, alongside the inhabitants, a number of exotic animals stroll by, including camels and giraffes.

More than fifty years later, Jacopo Tintoretto created for the same school *The Stealing of the Dead Body of St. Mark.* The removal of the body of the saint took place immediately after he was martyred when a sudden storm allowed the Christians of Alexandria to remove the stake on which he had been placed prior to cremation. The agitating action, which leaves the stake in the background, took place in a square not dissimilar to St. Mark's Square, with the Procuratie and the church of S. Geminiano once standing in front of the basilica while the exotic presence of the camel gently evokes Egypt.

At the end of the 15th century, Vittore Carpaccio also set his cycle of Scuola di Sant'Orsola in places where he had never been. With his vivid imagination he had no difficulty creating a far northern scene (Britain and Germany), often against the background of a Codussian Venice.

The story comes from *Legenda aurea* by Jacopo da Varagine, according to whom English ambassadors approached Ursula's father in Britain asking for the hand of his daughter on behalf of prince Ereo. After talking with her father, the girl accepted on the condition that Ereo be baptized at the end of a long pilgrimage to Rome. After the baptism, on the way back to Cologne, the couple ran into the king of the Huns who fell in love with Ursula. She strongly rejected the proposals of the bloodthirsty ruler, preferring instead inevitable death.

The story begins with the *The Arrival of the Ambassadors* in which a large room cut into sections is represented without background walls, while in the far background are buildings in Venetian taste with a hint of British landscapes.

Carpaccio was also summoned by the Scuola di San Giorgio degli Schiavoni (Dalmatians) to depict the cycles of Saint George and Saint Jerome, still *in situ*. In an episode of the cycle of Saint Jerome, he describes Saint Augustine in his study, where there are only two characters, the saint and a small dog; Saint Augustine told of being suddenly hit by a supernatural light while hearing the voice of Saint Jerome announce his death. The miracle is not obvious; one only sees the scholar looking enraptured towards the window in a silent room, where objects take on an almost symbolic connotation.

The cycle of Saint George is also taken from *Legenda aurea*, which narrates that Selene, a city in Libya, was oppressed by a terrible dragon that fed of the meat of the young and terrorized people with threats of death and destruction if it did not receive what it wanted. When it was the king's daughter's turn to be devoured, Saint George with his steed intervened swiftly and safely, injured the dragon and then led it into the town before killing it in front of everyone. Thanks to the surprise liberation from the nightmare, the knight persuaded the king and his people to receive baptism. In the combat scene with the dragon, the background is delineated to the left of the city, represented by several minarets, an obelisk, an equestrian statue, exotic palm trees and a castle typical of the Veneto region; on the other side is the African princess, dressed elegantly in European-style clothes, looking on with a frightened expression. In the foreground, Saint George struggles valiantly with the dragon on ground strewn with the remains of tortured bodies that symbolize the damage re-

The exterior of the Scuola Grande di San Rocco is defined by two different rows of Istrian stone.

Following pages, the Scuola Grande di San Rocco is known for a magnificent cycle of paintings created by Jacopo Tintoretto comprising more than 60 canvases.

Facing page,
Tintoretto, The Stealing of the
Dead Body of St. Mark,
1563-1564. Gallerie
dell'Accademia

Following pages,
the assembly room
at the Scuola Grande di San
Giovanni Evangelista
stands out for its polychrome
marble floor.

sulting from paganism, while the legendary animal represents the infidel who should be fought and converted.

Scuola Grande di San Rocco, which was founded in 1478, is the only one that still retains its functions, while all others were eliminated by a Napoleonic decree in 1797. Scuola Grande di San Rocco owes its luck to the fact that it contains the entire body of the saint of the same name, patron of plague-stricken; in the years when thousands of lives were annihilated by the plague, against which no real remedies existed, devotion held a key role. Because of this, the school was able to raise substantial funds with which it built the precious stone façade in Istrian stone designed by Antonio Scarpagnino, who took over after Bartolomeo Bon.

The decoration of the rooms was entrusted to Jacopo Tintoretto, who won the commission in an unusual way: when the competition was announced, and while participants were preparing their sketches, Tintoretto quickly, without anyone knowing, painted a large canvas. Probably with the complicity of some members, he installed it directly on the ceiling of the *albergo*. The cheeky gesture aroused much controversy but the painter was able to convince the brothers to give him the commission for the entire decorative cycle, realized in three distinct phases: the hall of the *albergo* from 1564-1567, the upper room between 1576 and 1581, and the hall on the ground floor from 1582 until 1587.

The iconographic program consists of scenes from the Gospel, the Old and New Testament. In this work Tintoretto demonstrated a unique and compact approach, using a limited palette with intense *chiaroscuro* effects. His canvasses are characterized by a bold, dynamic quality and unexpected perspectives and glimpses, which distance them from the serene Renaissance spatiality.

To obtain these unusual effects, the artist made use of models in wax or clay, dressed in drapes that he hung from the ceiling in order to study shadows and angle. He also built boxes in which he placed the characters, illuminating them with sources of direct light so as to explore the different plays of light.

CALLI, BRIDGES AND CANALS

Venice is made up of about a hundred islands separated by more than 170 canals and united by nearly 450 bridges. Its urban structure has remained almost the same through the centuries, as confirmed by a famous map by Jacopo de' Barbari, dated 1500, in which it is possible to recognise *campi* (squares), *campielli* (small squares), *calli* (narrow streets), canals, churches and buildings which still exist today. The city is divided into six areas called *sestieri*: San Marco, Castello and Cannaregio on one side of the Grand Canal and Santa Croce, San Polo and Dorsoduro on the other.

Local transit in Venice developed on land and water, two equally important routes which served different functions. The streets are comprised of *calli, campi, fondamenta* (wide quay) and bridges. Navigation, on the other hand, took place on the Grand Canal, the *rii* (small canals), the waterways which separate the individual islands and on the canals located beyond the city. These routes often follow sinuous and intricate paths, given that the construction of buildings and banks followed the contours of the islands in order to utilize the entire land surface.

Calli are the streets used by residents to walk to different locations in the city. They are sometimes wide but can be very narrow, allowing the passage of only one person at a time: some of them are called *ruga* when they are flanked by shops; others are called *salizada* because they were the first streets to be paved with slabs made from flint. The streets built over what once were canal tracts are called *rio terà*, while the *ramo* is a type of alley; a *piscina* is an area that used to be occupied by a pond; and *riva* and *fondamenta* are the banks that follow the canals.

Sometimes *calli* can carve out a little more space thanks to the *barbacani,* an architectural element also visible in the old streets of Damascus, demonstrating once again the close relationship between Venice and the East. These forms of reclamation are generally made of stone or wood: protruding from buildings about 70 centimeters toward the center of the street, one floor above ground level, they support the exterior wall of the house above the *calli* in order to leave more space for the traffic below.

In ancient times, traffic in the streets of the city center was very different from what we are accustomed to today. In the street, one could meet local residents, street vendors with their carts, foreign merchants, beggars, and a great number of horses, the most common means of personal transport among the higher social classes. The streets sometimes became so congested that a law was passed requiring mounts to be

Facing page,
Gentile Bellini, Miracle of the Cross at San Lorenzo Bridge, *1500. Gallerie dell'Accademia.*

*Facing page,
the Bridge of Sighs,
raised above the water
level, unites the Prisons
to the Doge's Palace.*

*Following pages,
the Rialto Bridge,
originally built in wood
with a central part which
could be raised, was rebuilt in
stone in the 16th century.*

equipped with bells in order to limit the number of accidents. At the end of the 13th century, four-legged animals were prohibited in areas where traffic was most intense, such as the Mercerie, the artery leading from St. Mark's Square to Rialto. In the 17th century, horses were confined to selected areas, including for example, one near the Calle Cavallerizza near Campo SS Giovanni e Paolo, which housed a stable, a sort of riding school. Wonderful performances took place there, in addition to representations of knightly tournaments and masked festivities for the entertainment of members of the nobility. The streets still carry their original names, often corresponding to names of saints of local parishes, names of aristocratic families residing in a particular street, or to the business activities that took place there. An example is found in the Rialto area, with its streets named Calle dei Varotari (tanners), Cordaria (ropes and wires), Ruga degli Speziali (spice vendors), Casaria (cheese), Naranzaria (oranges), Erbaria (vegetables), Pescaria (fish), and Beccaria (meat). By St. Mark's Square, one might instead venture onto a street named Spadaria (swords), Frezzaria (arrows), and Calle dei Fabbri (blacksmiths).

The city's toponomastics reflect a concentration of specialized activities, and bear witness to Venice's advanced economic organization, which guaranteed an ability to control prices for the benefit of citizens. The area between St. Mark's Square and the Rialto was the most visited teeming with the life and excitement commonly found in the heart of great European capitals. Wealthy businessmen and bankers rubbed shoulders with maid servants sent out on shopping errands, merchants dressed in exotic costumes and pancake vendors, while the cries of fishmongers, butchers and announcers of the latest news echoed around. Residents and visitors alike could find every type of entertainment

in the city center: from common taverns to comfortable inns; from restaurants to vendors of fried food and wine bars where good Greek wine was served; and from brothels to casinos and, later, prized coffee shops. In the midst of the crowd circulated the beggars, who, to be able to ask for alms, had to obtain a special license consisting of a sheepskin card sewn onto their clothes. Any fraudsters were sentenced to prison and subject to public flogging, while the boatmen who had brought beggars from the mainland were punished with the destruction of their vessel. The poor, however, were generally supported by various public and private charities.

The city awoke in the morning at eight during the summer and at ten during the winter. At sunset, the sound of *Realtina* (the Rialto bell) ended the workers' day, while those commercial activities which were not permitted to remain open throughout the night closed at nine o'clock in the evening. Streets were generally poorly lit; some corners escaped darkness thanks to the flame of oil lamps on small altars bearing sacred images, while the richest citizens employed servants who preceded them, illuminating the street with handheld lanterns. At the beginning of the 18th century, merchants began to hang lights outside their shops, making the streets in the centre safer, while lanters – the same kind used in the city of Paris – were introduced in 1732.

Originally the city was entirely built in wood, as were the bridges, formed by simple walkways that had mobile features, allowing the transit of vessels. But their lack of practicality led inevitably to changes, and soon the first wooden bridges were built with one or three arches, slowly replaced, as of the mid14th century, with structures made of stone. The first bridges featured no railings and were outiftted with wide, low steps to allow the passage of mounts. Once horses were no longer in use, and as a result also of numerous accidents, the

The Ponte dei Tre Archi takes on a rather uncommon form, one not generally used in the presence of rather wide canals.

first balustrades appeared towards the 18th century, while the first bridges in iron or cast iron appeared in the following century. It was precisely on the bridges without railings that a very popular game took hold in Venice between the 16th and 17th century. Known as 'wars on the bridges', it involved two rival factions, the Castellani and the Nicolotti, who exchanges punches and hit each other with sticks in order to conquer the central part of the bridge. However, the game often degenerated in dangerous ways. Participants hit each other hard, and sometimes the audience got involved hurling sharp objects. Not surprisingly, many competitors fell into the water, but some even lost their lives, crushed in the brawl or by drowning. Also for this reason, around the middle of the 18th century, the very popular fights were banned, leaving evidence of such events in the town

toponymy, such as the Ponte dei Pugni (bridge of Punches) at San Barnaba.

The bridges were the scene of other less violent games, such as the *Forze d'Ercole* (Strength of Hercules) where participants performed difficult balancing acts forming human pyramids that could reach up to eight people high. The game often ended in a general splash into the water for all in the canal below. At that time, the water was not as polluted as it is today. Because of the difficulty in finding drinking water, canal water had to be kept clean for domestic purposes. Due to this need, at the beginning of the 14th century, the government prevented the washing of clothes and the dyeing of wool in the canals. The law, which was often ignored but certainly limited the damage, was amended a century later by transferring all activities that produced hazardous waste – such as that

produced by dyers and butchers –, to the edges of the lagoon on the outskirts of the city, where a stronger tide could cleanse the water.

In modern times people move about using public transportation – the *vaporetti* (water buses). Once there had only been private vehicles, aside from the ferries. For centuries, the means of transport used by nobles and wealthy people was the horse, while the general public moved around on foot or by boat. While the use of horses remained popular until the 16th century, nobles gradually began to switch to the gondola, which, over time, became a true status symbol. In 1580, there were nearly 10,000 of these. Gondolas were covered by a sort of canopy with sliding windows, called *felze* which not only offered protection from the cold and rain but also allowed the passenger to travel in anonymity,

hiding stories of secret love affairs or clandestine meetings. The gondola's interior was variously decorated with finely embroidered velvets and silks, while the outside could be multi-colored, at least until the Magistrato alle Pompe, in order to quell the overly ostentatious display of luxury, imposed the color black. Passengers could enjoy a slow ride in a gondola, accompanied by the rhythmic sound of water splashing against the oar, while admiring the landscape, singing, playing instruments or playing cards.

The names given to places in Venice often allude to curious and picturesque stories or to news events of the time. A case in point is Riva di Biasio at S. Simeon Grande. At the beginning of the 16th century there dwelt and worked a sausage maker called Biagio Cargnio, known for the preparation of certain meat dishes. However,

The Ponte delle Guglie takes its name from four peaks that frame its extremities.

Preceding pages,
Accademia Bridge,
one of four that span
the Grand Canal, was rebuilt
in wood because it was consi-
dered temporary.

no one was aware that such dishes were made from the bodies of young children he had killed. One day a worker found a human finger bone in his dish and immediately alerted the authorities. Biagio ended up confessing his terrible crimes, and the Consiglio della Quarantia Criminale (Council of the High Court), the judiciary body responsible for punishing such crimes, sentenced him to a horrible end. He was first tied to a horse that dragged him from the court to his butcher's shop where his hands were cut off. He was then led in chains to St. Mark's Square between the two columns where he was quartered, after which the quarters were exposed for all to see, hung from the gallows. The house and shop were then razed to the ground so that nothing remained of him, but the story made such an impact on popular imagination that ever since then, that street on the Grand Canal has been known as the Riva di Biasio.

Another tragic story seems to have given the name to Ponte della Donna Onesta (bridge of the Honest Woman) at S. Pantalon. It is said that in a building overlooking the bridge lived a beautiful young woman married to a sword maker. A young nobleman took a shine to her and, in order to approach her, went to her house with the excuse of ordering a sword from her husband. After some time, he visited the house to check whether the weapon was ready and, finding the woman alone, brutally raped her. The young girl, filled with disgust and a sense of shame, took her own life with the same blade that her attacker had asked her husband to manufacture. But there is also another version of this story with a different ending in which a friend, alerted by the cries of the woman, rushed into the house and killed the attacker. Another kind of women, different from the virtuous wife of the sword maker, were the ones who worked in Calle delle Carampane at S. Cassiano. Since the mid 14th

century, a law provided that prostitutes should work in certain confined places concentrated in just one area for each district. In the district of S. Polo, a building formerly inhabited by the Rampani family was chosen for this purpose, hence the name Ca' Rampani. Access was denied after a certain hour and the building remained shut during on the days of the most important Catholic festivals. The house was run by matrons who, at the end of the month, divided the earnings among the prostitutes, also known by the name of the house as *carampane*. However, over time prostitution became increasingly tolerated and even recommended as a curative remedy due to the spread of sodomy, a practice that was fairly widespread since ancient times but decidedly opposed by Catholic morality and punishable by death. At Ca' Rampani, passersby could look at the scantily clad women, visible from the windows or door, and well lit by lanterns. As further evidence of the kinds of activities that took place in that area, just around the corner stands, above a canal, the Ponte delle Tette (bridge of Breasts). Although generally integrated into city life, prostitutes were subject to certain restrictions: they could not live in palaces on the Grand Canal or in overly luxurious houses; they were forbidden from traveling by boat or from entering church during the most solemn events; they could not dress in certain items of clothing typically worn by girls or wear pearls; and their testimony was not admissible in murder trials.

But bridges could also be the site of a miracle, as happened on the bridge of S. Lorenzo in 1369, according to tradition and admirably described by Gentile Bellini in his painting *Miracle of the True Cross at the Bridge of S. Lorenzo*. The confraternity of S. Giovanni Evangelista was heading towards the church of S. Lorenzo, as it did every year, when the reliquary of the Cross fell into the water but miraculously remained afloat, despite its considerable weight. Among the many who jumped into the canal to recover it, the only one who was able to retrieve the holy object was the Guardian Grande Andrea Vendramin. The name of the bridge Briati at the Carmini can be traced instead to a true story. Felice Briati was a bold Murano glassmaker who, in the first half of the 18th century, went to Bohemia to learn new techniques for working with glass. For centuries, the glassmakers of Murano worked with ancient and sophisticated secret methods and tried to fight the new Bohemian and English competition by remaining dedicated to traditional techniques. When Briati, having returned from his trip, began to apply his new knowledge, he aroused great dissatisfaction among his colleagues who ended up forcing him to leave the city. Some time after, however, he was able to return to Venice where he was allowed to open the first glassworks in a location other than Murano, precisely in the area of the bridge that now carries his name. The most famous and photographed bridge, besides Rialto, is certainly Ponte dei Sospiri (bridge of Sighs). It was built in 1600 to join Palazzo delle Prigioni (Prisons), erected a few years earlier, to the Doge's Palace in order to improve communication between the magistrates who administered justice. The condemned were transferred from court to the prisons across the bridge, which was built considerably higher than water level for security reasons. The view from the windows of the bridge is sublime: one can admire St. Mark's Basin, the island of S. Giorgio Maggiore and, in the distance, gaze at the open lagoon. Tradition has it that prisoners would glance at the landscape as they crossed the bridge, and utter a sad sigh, longing for their lost freedom.

Temporary bridges are also found in Venice. These include two votive bridges that for centuries have been set up each year on the anniversary of the vow made by the Venetian Republic, respectively, to Christ the Redeemer and the Virgin Mary, requesting an end to devastating plague epidemics. The first is the bridge of boats, 360 meters long, which leads from Zattere to the Redentore (the Redeemer) on the Giudecca, to enable the population to go on pilgrimages during the festival of the same name, every third Sunday in July. The second is linked to the temple of Madonna della Salute, built in 1630: since that year, every November 21, an 80-meter bridge is erected to join the opposite bank, and is crossed by thousands of worshippers. The longest bridge to be built was the railway bridge (about 3.5 kilometers long), built by the Austrians in 1841, almost fifty years after the fall of the Republic.

It radically changed the life of Venice, connecting the city to the mainland. From that day, Venice was no longer an island. Nearly a century later, a road bridge was built alongside the railway bridge, and took the name Ponte della Libertà (Freedom Bridge) at the end of the Second World War.

Following pages, the Bridge and Calle delle Tette stand where a famous brothel was once active.

Campi and Campielli

As already noted, in Venice there is just the one square, while all other open spaces are called campi, campielli or corti (courtyards), depending on their size. The campi (the word literally means fields) are so called because they were once pieces of land, partly cultivated or left to grow haphazardly (as indicated by the name of Madonna dell'Orto, or Madonna of the Vegetable Garden). For example, in the current Campo S. Salvador, there once flourished a grove of fig trees where the nobles tethered their horses before attending the meetings of the Great Council at the Doge's Palace. Even in St. Mark's Square, immediately opposite the basilica, was the *brolo*, a vegetable garden with vineyards.

The paving consisted of crushed earth for many years but it was later replaced by brick and then by *masegni* flint, a hard volcanic rock used initially in the most frequented areas and eventually used everywhere. As some 18th century prints show, in certain areas, (for example in Campo S. Stefano and Campo SS Giovanni and Paolo) only the central portion was paved while the remainder was left bare. The campo, surrounded by palaces, town houses, modest buildings and often by a canal, was the place where daily life took place, including that of the parish. Each campo housed a church in which members of the community gathered to celebrate the most important events: masses, baptisms, weddings and funerals. The campi were centers of activity for shows, festivals and a weekly market used by housewives or maidservants so that they could shop without having to go as far as the Rialto. A more peaceful atmosphere reigned in the campielli and courtyards where, during the summer season, the women brought out chairs, and occupied themselves with embroidery and small domestic jobs and chatting, while the children ran and played. The common feature of campi, campielli and courtyards was the presence of a well, leading to a constant stream of men and women equipped with buckets to carry a supply of drinking water.

The houses around the campi and along the canals were built using construction techniques that had remained virtually unchanged for centuries, including the use of a limited number of materials such as wood, brick and Istrian stone, which was highly resistant and easier to work with than marble. The peculiar geographical characteristics of the city: lying on a hard layer of clay that was not always compact and was prone to subsidence, dictated precise construction rules to counteract the continual settling of the land. Wood was employed in the joints and masonry, allowing structures a greater elasticity while distributing

Facing page,
in the small Campo San
Boldo, old paving stones
and Istrian stone meet
to create geometries.

weight in a uniform manner. Techniques used in naval construction were very helpful to address the stresses caused by the instability of the land, not entirely dissimilar to those generated by the sea.

In Venice, the availability of material was always a problem that was resolved in different ways. Wood generally came from the nearby woods of Dalmatia or from the mountainous areas north of the lagoon, arriving in the city through the rivers in the form of floating logs. The clay used to make the bricks and typical reddish color tiles was transported on large barges along the river Brenta. A more complex task was the transportation of stones, such as the red marble of Verona and Istrian stone (for the decoration of buildings) or flint (for paving) that came from far away, even a hundred kilometers at times.

The uniqueness of Venice was already apparent in its foundations, which required a sophisticated construction technique and the use of an impressive quantity of trees. The area to be built on was first made compact by means of a dense array of stakes planted within the soil in a concentric pattern starting from the perimeter walls. Two layers of boards were placed above this, and covered in turn up to the surface of the water with various layers of Istrian stone, the latter section taking on a slightly outward angular shape. This strong base was able to contain dampness and hold impressive walls. Only the stone and brickwork, depending on the sea tides, were periodically in and out of the water, while the stakes always needed to be covered, because without air contact, they underwent a chemical process that crystallized them. This made them extremely resistant, the foundation remaining intact even if another building was erected, such as when Baldassarre Longhena made use of the foundation of three pre-existing buildings for his grand project of Ca' Pesaro on the Grand Canal. The foundation required a

great number of poles, which consumed a large part of the budget for the construction of a building and also caused considerable ecological damage due to the massive deforestation it caused. Suffice it to say that for the basilica della Madonna della Salute alone, more than one million poles were used.

The larger campi have always been the place where celebrations, various kinds of entertainment and theatrical presentations have been organized. This is true in the case of Campo San Polo, the largest in the city, second only to St. Mark's Square. Surrounded by stately buildings, it was one of the most prized by the Venetians who were attracted by the various events and activities that took place there, such as the large market and target shooting with a bow and crossbow. Target shooting was an activity that was quite common in other areas, and was held in high esteem because it was not just entertainment but a real military exercise. In Campo San Polo, the public could also enjoy dancing, fireworks and especially bull hunts. This bloody game was very different from the risky Spanish bullfighting because instead of furious bulls, docile oxen were led into the campo where their horns were tied by ropes in opposite directions. Fireworks were placed on the animals' heads, to agitate them, and dogs were then unleashed to attack them. Depending on the occasion, from eight to twenty-four animals were sent into the fray. The stands were prepared on the day before the event for spectators, who would take their place after purchasing a ticket.

Campo San Polo was also the scene of an important international event: in 1547, Lorenzino de' Medici was murdered there with his uncle while he was leaving the house that he was renting in that area. Lorenzino had escaped across half of Europe after killing Alessandro de' Medici, Duke of Florence, and was hunted by the men of Cosimo, the successor to Alessandro. The

executors of the double murder on Campo San Polo, however, managed to escape the justice of the Serenissima thanks to the assistance of the Spanish ambassador who found a way to ensure their return home.

A campo with a history very different from the others is Ghetto Novo, surrounded by the houses of people belonging to the Jewish community. It consisted of rented residences because according to the laws of Venice, Jews could not own real estate, even if they were granted the right to convey the lease to their descendants or through marriage.

In 1516, Jews were confined to this area by a government decree. The Ghetto Novo was an island that was easily controllable because it was connected to the rest of the city by a single bridge. In the evening it was closed by two gates (whose hinges are still visible today) and at night the surrounding canals were patrolled by two boats, the cost of which was borne by the residents of the Ghetto.

While Jewish settlements had been built on the island of Giudecca as early as the 14th century, the origins of the Jews' presence in Venice is still not entirely clear. Historiography seems to accept that a permanent Jewish settlement existed as of 1382, when the High Council, concerned with the budgetary position of the Venetian Republic, decided to call upon money lenders in Venice, setting interest rates between 10 and 15 per cent.

The measure did not refer only to Jews

The Corte Morosini is characterized by a number of external staircases which once allowed access to the first floor of the residence.

Preceding pages,
Campo San Polo is the largest
in the city and was once the
scene of crowded markets and
colourful festivals.

but to providers in general. What distinguished Campo del Ghetto Novo from other areas of the city – and continues to do so today – is the absence of any church. Synagogues, sacred temples of the Ghetto, occupied the highest floors of the buildings, blending in with the residences. The term 'ghetto', which now generally refers to places of segregation, comes from the name of this island, *ghèto* (a dialect form of the Italian, '*getto*') that means "to cast" because of the existence of a foundry there. Despite the many limitations imposed by the government, Venice was really quite tolerant towards the Jewish community: in 1478 the decree of expulsion of 1426 was withdrawn. Thanks to the interest sparked by Jewish businesses, the community was able to enjoy the space it needed and express its religious and cultural identity. Many Jews decided to settle in Venice, and their number rapidly grew to 2,500 people on an island that could not expand; hence the only solution was to extend buildings upwards, at times reaching seven floors, three times more than the average for Venetian houses. Jews who remained in town for more than two weeks had to be distinguished from other citizens and were therefore required to wear a yellow badge. After a certain period, they were obliged to renew their residence permit by paying a fee.

The members of the community dedicated themselves profitably to their activities, in particular the lending of money with interest rates, which officially could not exceed a maximum of 15 per cent, and the sale of used items. In Campo del Ghetto many shops sprang up to sell various kinds of second-hand articles such as kitchen utensils, clothes, fabrics and furniture, and to rent furniture and luxury clothes. Jews were also not allowed to practice noble professions except that of the doctor. They were so appreciated as doctors that if called upon in an emergency, they were the only ones who were allowed to leave the Ghetto at night.

Over time, an improved relationship of cooperation between the Serenissima and the Jewish community was established, which led the latter to enjoy the freedom of practicing various occupations and engaging in international trade. An interesting example of this cooperation is that a project for the establishment of a Monte di Pietà, a pawn type loan institution of Franciscan origin, was rejected by the Great Council in 1778. The Monti di Pietà were formidable competitors for the money-lending work of Jews, and in the last quarter of the eighteenth century, there were more than seventy of these institutions on the mainland (with a turnover of over 5 million ducats a year).

A story that speaks instead of an all-Venetian merchant spirit is one that gives its name to the Corte del Milion, home to the famous traveler Marco Polo, who was born in Venice in 1256 to a family of merchants. Immediately following his birth, his father, Matteo, and his uncle, Nicola, set sail to explore new commercial opportunities in Asia. They returned there some time later with the young Marco, making one of the most amazing journeys in history, one that lasted twenty-five years. From Venice they reached Armenia, and upon crossing Iran, they traveled through the Gobi desert to reach Peking. Marco Polo received from the Great Kahn, the Mongol emperor, the official title that allowed him to travel and meet very developed and refined civilizations. He went to Japan, India and Siberia, and the Polo family, with their enterprising spirit, opened the silk route between Venice and China. Having emerged from his incredible adventures unharmed, a few years after his return home, during the war between Venice and Genoa, Marco Polo was captured and jailed by the Genoese. It is because of this period of imprisonment that we have one of the largest travel docu-

The Campiello delle
Stroppe shows the typical
conformation of a small
square with its numerous
access roads and a well.

ments of history, *Il Milione,* which Marco Polo dictated to his cellmate, recounting with accuracy and panache the beauty, the different socio-political systems and the curiosities of Asia.

Some campi took their name from the activities that were conducted in their space, as in the case of the Corte dei Cordami (Courtyard of Ropes) at the Giudecca. Atypical in size and configuration, it is surrounded by rows of houses in which lived the workers who were preparing the ropes for the ships. Its elongated shape relates to the requirement of the work, as hawsers had to be pulled and stretched to the utmost before being twisted. This courtyard is an interesting example of well-planned public housing, as seen also in other areas of Venice. The surrounding houses have a simple pattern and are rather widespread: on the ground floor was a room with a compacted earth floor where cooking and all other household tasks took place. In more recent centuries, a sink was added, which was directly linked to the bathrooms. Access to two rooms on the upper

Preceding pages,
Campo Santa Margherita
covers a large area,
surrounded by a parade
of differently-shaped
constructions
from different eras.

floor, used as bedrooms, was through a set of stairs which could be internal or external, and at least one of the rooms of the house enjoyed plentiful light thanks to a window that opened onto a canal, a garden or a courtyard. The description shows the superior housing conditions in Venice, where workers could enjoy a better quality of life than that experienced in other cities. Another kind of professional activity was exercised in Campo dell'Anatomia at San Giacomo dall'Orio where, in 1671, a school of anatomy opened, modeled after one in Padua that was in the form of a theater. A law in 1368 had already stipulated that each year studies of anatomy based on corpses should be carried out. These activities were also conducted in other places, but not on a systematic basis, due to opposition stemming from superstitions and popular belief.

Continuing with the medical theme, it is easy to trace the origin of the name of the Corte della Comare where, presumably, once lived a *comare*, the equivalent of a midwife. Since the 17th century, the government had set some standards for those who wished to practice this vital profession: the *comari* had to know how to read in order to study texts on pregnancy and childbirth; they had an obligation to attend at least two years of anatomy lessons related to their practice; and, prior to undergoing a demanding exam, they were required to have shadowed a "qualified" *comare* for at least two years.

Doctors also had to study and undertake a lengthy period of training before they could practice their profession. In the 14th century, the Republic employed twelve salaried doctors and surgeons, some of whom were specialized in particular diseases and called upon by other countries. Their work was supervised by the judiciary authority, which ascertained that they comply with specific rules, such as the requirement to meet every month to exchan-

ge views and information and to stay updated every year in the field of anatomy. Doctors were also strictly forbidden from prolonging the illness of patients for profit or from making special arrangements with pharmacists for speculative purposes.

An area known for the beauty of its monuments and as the scene of important ceremonies of the Doge is Campo SS Giovanni and Paolo, which owes its name to the church bearing the same name. Near the church, the magnificent equestrian statue of Bartolomeo Colleoni, a famous leader in the service of the Republic, dominates the campo. The statue is by Andrea del Verrocchio, who taught Leonardo da Vinci. While the fleet had always been led by a Venetian citizen, from the 14th century onwards, the army was headed by specialized mercenaries called *condottieri*, the name deriving from the *condotta*, or the binding contract which stipulated the salary and number of soldiers to be recruited. Once the terms of the contract had expired, the leader could continue on with another employer, but if he did so while he was still economically tied to someone else, he was considered a traitor. A tragic case was that of Carmagnola, who conquered for Venice the towns of Bergamo and Brescia, after which he remained inactive for a long time. This roused the suspicions of the Venetians who discovered that he had been recalled by his former client, the Duke of Milan. The inexorable Council of Ten then invited the *condottiere* to Venice in order to discuss which new strategies to put into practice. Carmagnola was received at the Doge's Palace with all honors but, as he was about to leave, was arrested and jailed. After being subjected to a trial, he was hung between the two columns in the Piazzetta.

Quite the opposite was the relationship between the Venetian Republic and Bartolomeo Colleoni, a shrewd businessman and valiant captain. Because of the lands

The Corte dei Cordami takes its name and elongated shape from activities it housed: ropes were stretched, pulled and then twisted.

Following pages, the vast Campo del Ghetto sits at the center of the area formerly reserved for Jews.

and treasures he obtained as fair payment for his work, he amassed quite a fortune. The leader left most of his assets to the Republic, asking in exchange to be immortalized by a monument in St. Mark's Square. However, the display of the image of an individual in the heart of the city was forbidden by decree. The government skirted around this issues by dictating that the statue be erected in front of the Scuola Grande di San Marco and close to the church of SS Giovanni and Paolo, where many notable Venetians were buried.

WELLS, PATERE AND CHIMNEYS

While important monuments and spectacular art works by the masters populate the Venetian landscape, many streetscape elements, large and small, have also survived over the years, blending harmoniously with their surroundings and serving as repositories of meaning, memories and customs. The wells found in every campo, campiello and courtyard are among the most widespread of such elements. Wells, formerly used to supply drinking water, were originally built as underground reserves to clean and conserve rainwater, and were constructed in a highly functional manner. Nearly six meters deep and waterproofed with a coat of clay, they collected water that streamed down through holes made at the four corners of the surrounding area.

Rainwater flowed through several brick channels and was filtered by seeping through river sand, eventually reaching a circular central tank, also made of brick, where it was collected with a bucket lowered from the mouth of the well. During hard times of drought, barges transported water from mountain springs along both the Brenta and the Sile rivers. Today's drinking water comes through a long aqueduct that begins around twenty kilometres inland and runs along Ponte della Libertà, the bridge that connects Venice to the mainland. The tanks' visible part are the wellheads – usually made of Istrian stone and more rarely in marble – decorated depending on the era in which they were constructed and according to the patron's taste. They were manufactured with high quality standards and finely carved with exquisite workmanship. Certain ancient wells, such as those dating back to early Christian times, are cylindrically-shaped and decorated with fantastical animals and stylized motifs, while those built in the Veneto-Byzantine style display twisted columns and animals. During the Renaissance, polygonal shapes with masks, heads, garlands and cherubs began to make an appearance (most notably, from the 15th century, the red marble of Verona wellhead in the courtyard of the Ca' d'Oro, and the 16th century wellhead of Campo SS Giovanni e Paolo). In the Baroque years, wells were decorated with capitals with rich volutes, while in the Neoclassical period they featured an essential and linear structure. Some wellheads were privately owned and placed in the courtyards of the nobles' homes, but most of them were public and accessible to everyone.

The construction of a well involved a considerable expenditure, which was only sporadically assumed by the State. An

Facing page,
Vittore Carpaccio, Miracle of the Relic of the Holy Cross at the Rialto Bridge, *1496.*
Gallerie dell'Accademia

example of a major intervention by the State relates to a dry summer during the first half of the 15th century when following three months of drought, the authorities decided to dig thirty new wells to increase water reserves. The wells built by the State bore the effigy of the lion of St. Mark while the coats of arms of noble families defined those constructed with private funds. Often noble families assumed the task of providing water to the neighborhood as a charitable act, one among many that the State suggested to the ruling class.

The area surrounding wells was typically swarming with housewives, domestic servants, apprentices and shopkeepers, going noisily about with buckets and various containers in order to supply water for drinking, cooking and occasionally for washing. In ancient times, in Venice as in other cities, cleansing the body did not have the same meaning as it does today, and the use of water for this purpose was rare even among the high social classes.

Occasionally wells could also offer some strange surprises: on June 14, 1779, a young maidservant tossed her bucket into the well of San Trovaso, only to pull up a human torso. The city's horror at the gruesome discovery increased after the discovery of two legs in a campo nearby and a head floating in a canal the next morning. The judiciary authority arranged for the head to be embalmed and displayed, in the hope that someone may recognize the person. Investigations to find the murderer took a different turn when a letter signed with initials was found on the body. This evidence led investigators to the brother of the deceased, who identified the body and led authorities to the wife of the victim who had often complained to his brother that his wife was having an extramarital affair. Investigations were concluded when the woman and her lover confessed to having murdered her husband in order to marry freely.

Stone mcdallions embellished with bas-reliefs of plants or animals, known as *patere*, were widespread throughout Venice. While their function was less pragmatic than that of the wells, they still played an important role. Derived from the ancient East and mounted on the façades of houses and on courtyard walls, these decorative elements enjoyed a certain popularity for centuries due to their figurative representation of two easily understandable concepts: good and evil. The reliefs, with images of Christ or of a strong animal triumphing over an 'evil' one, such as an eagle killing a snake, symbolized the power of virtue over vice, while representations of negative symbols, such as demons or sirens, probably had an apotropaic function.

Over time the reliefs lost their symbolic meaning but remained to enrich the streets of the city, along with many other decorative and commemorative elements as testimony of past beliefs and values. One such example is the tile placed at the entrance of the Mercerie depicting the tale of an old woman who, at the beginning of the 14th century, accidentally dropped a piece of mortar on the head of a standard-bearer. He was boldly leading a squadron of armed men towards St. Mark's Square to support Bajamonte Tiepolo in his plot against the Doge. Tradition narrates that the rebels, after the incident, became discouraged and were sent fleeing by the Doge's soldiers.

In Campo dei Mori in Cannaregio, three niches carved into the wall of a building contain the statues of three men with turbans who tell another ancient story. The tale is one of three wealthy brothers who came from Morea to live in Venice where

Left,
A bas-relief of a camel
at Palazzo Mastelli is one
of the many decorative
elements that tell the story
of the city.

Right,
The winged lion, symbol
of Venice, is often found
on state buildings of
the Republic.

Following pages,
The Gothic courtyard
of Ca' d'Oro is made in
brick, decorated in Istrian
stone, and graced by a
prized wellhead.

they built their houses. One is the house that is generally known as Palazzo del Cammello because of the bas-relief of a camel led by a man wearing an eastern-style headdress.

Different kinds of figures – such as bearded, severe faces or lion's heads – can be found on the keystones of the portals of town houses and on Istrian stone lintels and cornices between calli, campi, and campielli. Carved around the 16th century, they became, over time, increasingly theatrical and grotesque, exhibiting an unusual play of *chiaroscuro*. On the other hand, terrifying stone faces guarded the doors of bell towers and served the purpose of keeping out the devil. Sacred themes permeated the city: statues, bas-reliefs, or pictures of the Madonna, Christ or the saints were found on the walls of houses and palaces, in niches or under small roofs.. These diminutive altars existed as early as the beginning of the 12th century and by law had to be lit, especially in the darker areas of the city, in order to make the roads safer. They were generally looked after by the lord of the area, who sometimes shared the task with the State.

As with the *patere*, these features also had esoteric value: while safeguarding residents from the hazards of the night, according to popular belief they could also be effective against the plague, and some people even said they could work miracles. Today, they still have spiritual significance for believers who venerate them with offerings, flowers and prayers.

But the most important theme of the Venetian territory is, without a doubt, the lion of San Marco, the symbol of Venice, whose main attributes are wings and a book. The lion may take the form of a *moeca*, whose round shape recalls that of the crab (the *moeca* is one of the stages of transformation of the crab when, in its molting phase, it loses the old shell and a soft shell appears, the so called *moeca*, which then thickens and becomes a new form of armour), or it can be a *leone passante*. In the latter case, the lion stands with the book held in one of the front paws. The book, which in representations from the Gothic period was normally closed, began to appear open during the Renaissance and in subsequent centuries. There is no foundation to the popular myth that the book was closed in times of war and open in times of peace.

While the shape and size of the *leone in moeca* makes it well suited to be encased on keystones, in entablatures, and within ceilings, the *leone passante* makes a proud display on the façades of public buildings, on portals and on walls.

Unfortunately most of St. Mark's lions were systematically destroyed upon the fall of the Republic in 1797, yet many still remain, having escaped the Napoleonic devastation. These include a 16th century lion on the clock tower in St. Marks'

This page,
the statues on the walls
of Campo dei Mori depict two
men in turbans, two
of three brothers who came
from Morea.

Facing page,
view on the Fondamenta dei
Mori. Fondamenta is a path
that runs alongside a canal.

Square, as the lion that dominates the entrance of the Arsenale, and less significant ones on wells and public bridges. Each lion relates to a piece of the city's past: from the ones that proudly represent the Republic at strategic points of the city, to the *leoncino dei frustai* carved at Rialto in the 16th century, where those sentenced for a crime would kiss it before being whiplashed.

When lifting one's gaze to the roofs, the panorama of Venice assumes a particular tinge of red, typical of the tiles which cover the city. The dominant element, in addition to the aerials, are the picturesque chimneys. These come in many styles: barrel-shaped, square sectioned, and bell-shaped, with openings at the sides, and cylindrical.

In some cases, two or more chimneys blend into a single body in a bilobal or trilobal section. Often the chimneys take the shape of a truncated cone to allow the sparks to fall back down and inwards, thereby removing the risk of fire, which, in the past, was the worst threat in Venice. In ancient times, many chimneys were painted with vivid colors that blended harmoniously with the colours of the façade, expressing the personality of the owner of

Patere are stone tiles carved with vegetable and animal motifs.

the house. One can get an idea of how the most beautiful chimneys in the 15th and 16th centuries looked from the detailed paintings of Gentile Bellini and Vittore Carpaccio or from watching the enchanting forest of vertical flues on the roof of certain buildings, including Ca' Dario, famous for the precious façade of inlaid coloured marble that overlooks the Grand Canal.

Construction of chimneys demanded special care even in public housing. Characteristic chimneys are found more or less everywhere, and a prime example are those of the so-called House of the Seven Chimneys, a specimen of terraced houses which had been part of Venice's landscape since the most ancient times. Here the flue was built outside the building and is therefore clearly visible, its funnel shape often conferring a characteristic look to the façades of buildings. Inside the palaces, chimneys were built into side walls for practical and aesthetic reasons. In the simplest houses, the fireplace was located in the kitchen and was at the center of domestic life; in aristocratic homes, fireplaces were in the side rooms, where residents lived, while the central hall, the *portego*, was only a place of transit in everyday life. Impressive and much higher than the chimneys were the obelisks on the roofs of some palaces, standing as proof that in the past, the building was the residence of an admiral or sea captain (such as Palazzo Balbi or Palazzo Tiepolo Papadopoli).

Another famous characteristic of the elevated panorama is the *altana* (roof terrace), probably originating from the Middle East. This is a terrace located above the roof of the house, supported by pillars that hold up the floor boards and is enclosed by wooden or iron balustrades. In a city where space for gardens is limited, the *altana* becomes a valuable outdoor space, to enjoy cool evenings during the summer and to hang laundry to dry. In the past, the roof was even more appreciated, especially by ladies who did not have many opportunities to go out, except to go to Mass or to a reception.

Women and girls met on the *altane* to talk, embroider and lighten their hair (during the 16th century, women coveted *biondo*

Tiziano flowing hair, named after the golden hair color of women depicted in the paintings of the great Venetian artist Titian).

Ladies wore wide-brimmed hats to protect them from the sun and thus avoided the unwanted suntan, typically associated with poor social classes who were forced to work outdoors. However, this was no ordinary headwear: in fact, it had a hole in the center and did not protect the top of the head from the sun, resulting in bleached hair when specific substances used on the hair would interact with sunlight.

There were various and interesting recipes for tinctures which made use of different substances such as sulfur, eggs and orange peel mixed with liquid compounds.

The House of Seven Chimneys is an example of row houses built in Venice since earliest times.

Following pages, left, Campiello del Remer with a typical well that supplied drinking water. Right, Corte Botera, the visible part of the cisterns is built from wellheads mostly made of Istrian stone.

*Detail of the façade
of Ca' Dario entirely
decorated in polychrome
marble and stones
cut into disks.*

*The chimneys of Ca' Dario
take the shape of truncated
cones, to allow the sparks
to go back into the opening.*

*Following pages,
around the Campo della
Maddalena one can see
the different forms that
chimneys can take:
reed-like, square-section,
bell shaped with side
openings, and cylindrical.*

Similar to hair care, care of one's body was also held in high regard. Women could spend hours in front of a mirror to comb their hair, lengthen eyelashes, color the cheeks and even the cleavage.

To make the skin softer, they would sleep at night with slices of veal that had been left immersed in milk for hours and used other extravagant recipes for bleaching teeth, the skin of hands and feet, coloring nails and perfuming the skin. It was also common practice to make clothing fragrant through the use of pleasant smelling balls, and everything was contained in bags and boxes, such as those for coins or the rosary.

The most popular substances include musk, amber, aloe, mint and myrrh. The great profusion of fragrant water also had a therapeutic value: for example, melissa and macerated musk in wine were considered infallible remedies against heart disease, and soap in the form of pills was used against headache and chest pain. In the 16th century, however, personal hygiene was a rather marginal factor. Patrician houses had no bathrooms that would fit with our current definition, and baths were taken in the bedroom in prized but rather small basins.
Some preferred bathing in wooden tubs containing little water, but liberally doused with perfumes.

GARDENS

The gardens of Venice are, for the most part, hidden behind high walls, giving visitors the impression that it is a city made of stone and water.

In reality, an aerial view of the lagoon shows green areas are more common than generally perceived, though they are significantly fewer in number than those represented in the famous map by Jacopo de' Barbari of 1500. In the distant past, a large portion of the islands making up Venice was comprised of agricultural land, woods and cattle grazing fields. When large-scale buildings were built on the archipelago, the number of green areas progressively diminished. By the 13th century the economy of the Serenissima was based principally on international trade, a factor that led to a progressive relocation of agricultural activities to nearby inland territories. The concept of the garden is, in any case, relatively recent. Smaller parcels of land, often situated behind houses and surrounded by walls, consisted for the most part of vegetable plots used to cultivate fruit and vegetables to meet the needs of individual families, and then sell any surplus produce. The first gardens were expressly designed for the cultivation of medicinal plants which were then dried, treated, mixed and sold by pharmacists in chemist shops. The work of these pharmacists – under state supervision, which guaranteed a certain level of professionalism – provided high quality products which helped to maintain a monopoly. The chemist shops of the Serenissima soon became meeting places where scientists from all over Europe exchanged information relating to remedies, experiments, tests and alchemic research. Beginning in the 16th century, these scientists could refer to scientific texts from printed books rich in thoroughly detailed illustrations, which became essential instruments for the study of curative herbs. During the same period, the Botanical Garden of Padua, an important scientific laboratory with links to the University, was also established. This passion for officinal plants also involved many citizens, such as the famous Pier Antonio Michiel, whose garden in San Trovaso, which no longer exists, became one of the most famous in Venice. His interest in plants led to this nobleman, who was in constant contact with others who shared the same passion, becoming a great expert in botany.

These experts exchanged information, seeds, and drawings and often asked ambassadors or merchants who traveled to distant lands to bring exotic specimens back with them. The most detailed and complete plant catalogue known since the 16th century is credited to Michiel, whose scrupulous descriptions accompanied accurate drawings of 1,000 botanical spe-

Facing page,
the Gardens of the Biennale
are part of an extensive
complex of green spaces,
designed in the 19th century.

Gardens in Venice are often hidden behind high boundary walls which merely hint at their presence.

cies. The small Venetian garden, a secluded medieval *hortus conclusus*, surrounded by battlemented walls, also became a place for meditation, silence, reading and amorous encounters. Medicinal essences, allotment plants and hedges filled its borders according to precise rules. A notable example is the garden of Ca' Dario, whose perimeter and structure have remained unchanged even though the plants are no longer the same as the original ones. In pa-

laces, the gardens were often separated from the building by a courtyard, an area used to carry out of various domestic chores. During the Renaissance era, the garden became a decorative feature in which plants were arranged according to studied plans in order to create artificial scenes. Instead of cultivating plants with curative properties and fruit, owners began to collect botanical species that would guarantee a sufficient chromatic variety in

all seasons or that would lend themselves to unusual pruning, such as box trees, laurels and myrtles.

The gardens also contained classic style statues and displayed architectural elements such as open galleries or pergolas with barrel vaults. Perimeter walls were hidden by evergreen climbers, rose plants and jasmine or embellished with objects, such as shells, bone fragments or colored glass, or even coral and mother-of-pearl.

For the frequent social events that were organized during the times, ravel and decorative sand were painted in different shades, a practice that was even extended to the coloring of flower petals. This exquisitely Manneristic trend for the artificial was widely popular in the second half of the 16th century. In the gardens of the wealthy, walls were concealed by spectacular frescoes, which reproduced the floral motifs of the area or represented fantastic lan-

View from above of a garden with its fine geometry of flower beds and gravel paths.

dscapes. At times, the garden became a magnificent private stage, outlined by sophisticated backdrops in cloth, where spectators could enjoy comedies and listen to concerts. Almost none of these ancient splendors have survived; only a few fragments remain, along with detailed descriptions from manuscripts of the period.

Venetian gardens are still characterized by their small size and flat layout, due to the morphology of the archipelago. These factors contributed in part to a somewhat monotonous configuration that was in contrast to the elaborate Italian-style gardens, to be found around the country, with their terracing, rigorous geometry and views overlooking vast areas. To protect them from being submerged by the brackish water of the lagoon during high tide, small gardens were initially placed on a slightly raised area with a central axis formed by a small gravel path. Over the centuries, and due to climactic factors, plants such as laurels, hackberries, yew and boxwood hedges became a common feature, and are still present today.

By contrast, on the islands of Murano and Giudecca, the nobles built their holiday house gardens on vast lands, decorating and embellishing them with lush fruit trees and vines, along with classic architectural elements. It was here that owners and their guests devoted themselves to a wide range of pastimes, from receptions to imaginative and recreational horse rides. In the game of the market gardener, for example, members of the aristocracy, dressed as gardeners, would spend hours discussing flowers as representations of feelings. This symbolic language was based on colors, in which white represented trust in a loved one, green symbolized hope, yellow stood for desperation, blue for jealousy, red for revenge and orange for joy.

One of the most beautiful gardens of the Giudecca belonged to the immensely wealthy Pisani family and was a stage for im-portant social events, such as the visit of Gustav III of Sweden in 1784. In preparation for the party, a famous theatrical set designer was called upon to adorn the garden. A large room was constructed facing the lagoon, equipped with an air conditioning system made from containers filled with ice, which were continuously replaced. The walls of the garden were decorated with canvas featuring flowers and plants, while transparent crystal fruit, lit from within, hung from the trees. A theme of flowers and fruit ran through the entire scenario with a profusion of color, scents and sensations.

A flatboat floated on the lagoon carrying a structure similar to an arc de triomphe which was completely illuminated, and from which reflections were multiplied by a series of artfully mounted mirrors.

Almost nothing remains of those imaginative gardens: only the vegetable plots of the church del Redentore and the garden of Villa Eden can still be seen today. Eden, the owner and the person for whom the garden is named, restored it to its original appearance in the times of the Serenissima at the end of the 19th century.

The 1800s brought a revival of interest in botany, and people resumed cultivating exotic plants on private lands in an almost scientific manner, bringing new vitality to many of the semi-abandoned gardens.

In the 19th century, the new English gardening style introduced major changes and enhancements to the most extensive green spaces. The new romantic garden had an irregular shape and was characterized by many different elements, and an unusual variety of panoramic views.

Assorted elements were carefully placed within the space, including small wooded areas, colorful flowerbeds, pergolas covered with climbers, such as roses and fragrant jasmine, and hedges. Other accents included sculptures, pots, architectural elements, obelisks, small bridges and tur-

This is one of the rare
gardens that face out onto
the Grand Canal, a splash
of green barely separated
from the water.

Following pages, left,
facing over a secondary
canal, this lush garden is
edged with cypress trees,
an element typical of the
Romantic era.

On the right, typically
the green area is dedicated
to pleasure, and is connected
to the building via a
courtyard that was formerly
the center of domestic
activities.

rets, lodges and huts. Among the informal gardens that can still be seen today are the gardens of Palazzo Gradenigo (now in a completely overgrown state) and the garden of Palazzo Albrizzi at Sant'Aponal, which despite its small size, still retains a vaguely romantic atmosphere, with a little bridge that connects it to the palace and the Neo Gothic tower. The most extensive Papadopoli and Savorgnan public gardens are very different from their original 19th century styles. Immediately after the fall of

*Garden overlooking
the Grand Canal decorated
with an impressive arch
in Istrian stone.*

the Republic, Gian Antonio Selva designed the public gardens of Castello. The
project involved the clearing of a large part
of the area but almost none of the planned
service buildings were constructed. From
1887, the Biennale di Venezia occupied
roughly two thirds of this lush territory. In
the first stages, the Padiglione Italia was
built for exhibition purposes and was later
followed by other foreign pavilions.

The Royal Gardens, commissioned by Napoleon, occupied the area facing the basin
of St. Mark's from which sprang the Gra-
nai della Repubblica, the building of the
ancient granaries of the Venetian Republic. Fondazione Querini Stampalia has
one noteworthy garden, designed by the

Venetian architect Carlo Scarpa at the end
of the 1950s. This space is dominated by a
rigorous geometry defined by the insertion
of a number of austere cement partitions
set within the verdant grassy carpet, four
different trees and thin water ponds.

From the 16th century forward, the dominant position of the Serenissima was gradually compromised by shifting trade routes caused by a new balance of power within the Mediterranean, including the formation of large European states and the
discovery of America. Venetians therefore
were forced to diversify their traditional
activities, becoming receptive to new inve-
stments and to the acquisition of lands in
the nearby inland areas. Such economic in-

terets grew in parallel to landowners' desire to build new holiday residences, which eventually became sumptuous villas surrounded by splendid parks, many of them still intact to this day.

In the 1700s, these holiday retreats became an established tradition and members of the aristocracy competed with each other to enhance their second residences.

In terms of their exterior magnificence and their interior opulence, the countryside retreats often exceeded the owners' town houses. In the countryside, owners were finally able to freely indulge their fantasies and vanities.

In their parks and gardens, they created a celebration of botanical variety, accentua-

ted by lakes, lemon groves, rabbit hutches, gazebos, mazes, fishponds and huts. Aristocratic families retreated to the countryside in the summer when the temperature in the city became suffocating, departing with trunks and servants following days of intense preparations. Venetians reached the villas on the banks of the river Brenta by taking the *Burchiello*, a ship that moved along the river pulled by horses, while others took carriages.

During the holidays, days were spent walking through nature, reading enjoyable books, accepting invitations to lunch, games and shows in the garden, and conversing in crowded cafes.

A garden partly covered by creepers and crossed by a pergola held up by white columns.

Following pages, the central part of this garden is defined by a finely-carved well which is located at the meeting of the paths.

ARSENAL

As in the Venetian arsenal is seen / in winter, the tenacious pitch to boil, / to tar the unsound vessels o'er again, / and the meanwhile, / one makes a vessel new, one recaulks now / ribs that have known much of sea-voyage toil; / one hammers at the stern, one at the prow, / this one makes oars, and that one twists the twine, / and one doth mainsail or the mizzen sew; / thus not by fire, but by an art divine, / a dense pitch down below was boiling here/which made the bank on all sides viscid shine. / This did I see, but in it I saw there / Nought but the bubbles which the boiling raised, / How all did swell, then falling compressed appear.

(Translated by Charles Tomlinson, 1877)

Above is the description Dante Alighieri produced of the Arsenal (shipyard) of Venice after visiting it in 1312. He was so impressed by it that he included it in his *Divina Commedia* (*Divine Comedy*) in the Canto XXI of the *Inferno*, comparing it to the bedlam in which *barattieri* (grafters) are immersed in boiling tar. The shipyard was still young during Dante's time. It was to become the most important one in the world, and had taken shape as a result of incessant activity, amidst tar fumes, the rasping of saws and of the pulling of cords, the din of nails being hammered and oars being filed, the creaking of carts and the cries of men shouting orders.

It was a perfect machine that formed the basis of wealth and prestige of the Serenissima. The instruments that allowed Venice to prevail on the seas were constructed in the Arsenal: the powerful armada that for centuries had defeated the enemies who arrived from across the Mediterranean; and the merchant ships, capable of systematically outclassing the competition encountered in both nearby and distant ports. Between 1,000 and 2,000 men worked there, with an internal organization that made it an *ante litteram* industrial centre and that occupied an eighth of the area of the city. Around 1560, it covered an area of around 250,000 square meters and employed about two thousand men. Lane highlights how, at that time, the Arsenal was "the greatest factory of Christianity and perhaps throughout the whole world".

Traditionally, Venice was dotted with private *squeri* (boat yards) where small boats were manufactured alongside large ships, but a large part of the construction work was carried out in the Terranova shipyard, situated on the wharf near the Doge's Palace. In the 13th century, the new State shipyard, the Arsenal, was established in a marshy area inhabited by few people. At the start, the complex was probably only

Facing page,
Paolo Veronese, Allegory of the Battle of Lepanto, *1572.*
Gallerie dell'Accademia.

The Arsenal, expanded
to occupy one-eighth
of the city, was surrounded
by walls interspersed
by 15 towers.

used for docking and warehousing, but other activities were soon added. In a brief time, the new facility came to replace the Terranova shipyard. The latter was eventually discarded, probably because it caused excessive traffic in a central area of the city. In its place arose the great building of the State Granaries, where wheat reserves were stocked, to be sold at a modest price during periods of famine.

The new shipyard was strategically located near the mouth of the port, a site protected by the forts that blocked the enemies' access and at the same time allowed ships to quickly set sail. The Arsenal was constructed in a natural bay that was deep enough to allow the presence of large dock ships. It was initially constructed from two rows of warehouses, clearly visible on the plan by Jacopo de' Barbari of 1500. Later it was extended, encompassing a basin of water

and in the 15th century it became even larger with the construction of another section: the Arsenale Novissimo. Other additions were made at a later date, designed by some of the most famous architects of the time.

In the 16th century, Antonio Da Ponte, the architect who would soon thereafter plan the Rialto Bridge, reshaped for the production of rope the Corderie della Tana, a very long building measuring 315 meters (and 20 meters wide), supported by 84 stone columns. The extraordinary size was dictated by production requirements, given that some of the sails, anchors and moorings were extremely sizeable. Depending on the purpose, the lines were in canopy or cotton, a raw material originating from Tana, the city on the Black Sea that gave its name to the construction.

The Gaggiandre area, a covered stretch of

water for construction activities that were carried out directly on the water, is attributed to Jacopo Sansovino while in 1555, Michele Sanmicheli, the Mannerist architect renowned for his military constructions, planned a shed for the boathouse of the precious *Bucintoro*. The building, both simple and majestic, shows a precious rusticated facade made from elements of a Doric order. The *Bucintoro* was the luxurious boat of the Doge, entirely gilded and engraved. It was used for important ceremonies on the water, such as the famous Festa della Sensa, the 'wedding with the sea'. Barbarously torn apart as a sign of disrespect during the French occupation, a model of the *Bucintoro* can today be seen in the Historical Naval Museum.

The victories of Venice's fleet began around the year 1000 thanks to the important commercial privileges granted to the city by the Byzantine emperor who, in exchange for military assistance, conceded licences, shops and warehouses in the strategic port of Constantinople. Furthermore, the Venetians, by now famous worldwide for the excellence of their construction activities, were commissioned the galleys for the Crusades, the rent of which was paid with important concessions in the conquered ports. In the 15th century, the Republic could count on the strongest fleet in Southern Europe and used it to bolster its commercial activities, a fundamental aspect of its power.

In the Arsenal the construction of ships continued at an unrelenting pace: faster ships for war, roomier ships for the market. The Venetians were able to amaze foreigners with their incredible speed in fitting out the ships. The king of France, Henry III, on an official visit to the lagoon,

The shipyard was entirely surrounded by crenellated walls, had only one land access point, and at night the doors were always closed.

Following pages, the extraordinary dimensions of many interiors, such as the Corderie, were dictated by production needs.

*The Gaggiandre, attributed
to Jacopo Sansovino, are
water-based shiyards
dominated
by impressive arches.*

was surprised to learn that the arsenalotti (shipyard workers), in just one hour, had assembled, equipped and launched a galley, which had been prepared to meet his royal requirements.

Even more formidable was the speed and the perfect organization with which the arsenalotti in 1570 prepared the fleet for the battle of Lepanto, a decisive defeat against the Turks for domination of the Mediterranean. In only 50 days, 100 "ships on standby" were equipped with main masts, anchors, sails, ropes, sails, cannons, various arms and food supplies. The galleys that set sail from the Arsenal were joined by those that had docked in other Venetian ports. Venice and its allies returned victorious with a booty of 117 ships and thousands of prisoners. This victory against the infidels and the competitors in the Medi-

terranean culminated in a critical moment for the fate of Venice which was already showing the first signs of decadence. This important event was repeatedly celebrated and immortalized, for example in the famous painting *Allegory of the Battle of Lepanto* by Veronese in the Gallerie dell'Accademia.

The capacity to build or fit out a considerable number of ships in a short timespan was the result of meticulous and prudent planning. Up to 150,000 oars, 5,000 benches, an incredible length of rope and hundreds of canons could be stored and be ready for use in the warehouses; the tasks of the arsenalotti were organized exactly as in a production line.

Often the boats were not constructed according to any particular design or plan but developed in an empirical manner, the

result of a natural evolution, based on in-depth technical knowledge. Two types of sailing ships were essentially produced in the Arsenal. The first was galleys, streamlined boats and light first *triremi* (galleys with three rows of oars on each side) and then *quinquiremi* (with five rows of oars), that were extremely maneuverable also on days of little or no wind, and capable of transporting a large crew fitted out for a sea attack. The second was rounded boats, much heavier and more capacious, which could store a great quantity of goods.

Since ancient times, merchant ships had generally been owned or rented by a group of business men, often noblemen belonging to the same family. From this group derives the name of this type of company: *fraternal* or *colleganza*. It was a system that allowed the equal distribution of earnings and risk. In the *colleganza*, some of the members supplied the capital and others the work, which was generally carried out in the ports which that were already known, such as Constantinople and Cyprus. From these locations, it was easy to maintain an epistolary relationship in order to issue orders to the agent and to stay up to date with the situation and any variations in prices.

Within the ship construction site, technical and administrative responsibility was assigned to the three Lords of the Arsenal who, beginning in the 16th century, were supported by the Admiral, a veritable technical-industrial director. The arsenalotti who were employed by the state did not receive a particularly high salary but they belonged to a protected category that was entitled to concrete guarantees. As a sign

The architecture of the hangars reflects the function of the Arsenal as an industrial center that was ahead of its times.

*Facing page,
the Arsenal was built
around a natural basin,
and its architecture can
be reflected on the calm
waters of the lagoon.*

*Following pages,
this water entry is bound by
two towers, and opens out onto
a canal that is spanned by a
bridge which could
formerly be raised.*

of the importance conferred upon their role, during ceremonies they occupied a prominent position and it was these same workers who followed the Doge immediately after his election and who carried his coffin at his funeral. The State also took care of these individuals, as in the case of the young man who died while trying to extinguish the fire at Fondaco dei Tedeschi (German Warehouse). The arsenalotti assumed the role of fire fighters until the 18th century, at which time an autonomous fire fighting operation was established. The Government assigned a lifetime payment to the widow and son of 8 soldes a day, a sum corresponding to the young man's salary. In similar cases, if the heir was male, he was offered a job that was guaranteed at the Arsenal; if the heir was female, she could depend upon a dowry, without which she would not have been able to marry.

In return for this protection, the State expected the arsenalotti to carry out demanding work that was strictly regulated. Evidence of the Government's tight regulatory grip is given by an episode that occurred in the 16th century, when workers learned they would not longer be paid for working on Saturday afternoon, due to the number of hours lost while waiting in the queue to be paid. A protest march made its way to the Doge's Palace; the dispute was rapidly suppressed and resulted only in the heads of the uprising being put into prison for several months. In any case it had been unthinkable in the past that any authority would give in to the demands of employees.

Hours were inflexible: the entrance bell sounded for half an hour and if any employee arrived at the Arsenal once the chimes of the entrance bell had ceased, he would lose the equivalent of one day's pay. Similarly to other artisans, arsenalotti also formed corporations or schools that disciplined professional conduct in their line of work. Initially, shipyard workers were divided into three schools: the *marangoni* (carpenters), the *calafati* (sealers) and the sail sewers. Enrolment with a scuola represented a kind of insurance that guaranteed, among other things, a life payment for the disabled, financial support for orphans, dowries for daughters at an age when they could marry and the coverage of funeral expenses. A type of pension was also envisaged which offered the elderly the possibility of continuing to work. Shipowners were in fact obligated to include in their journeys a man older than fifty-five for every six sailors employed. It was stipulated that apprentices should not be younger than twelve or older than fourteen, with the exception of sons of the masters who could be taken on at the age of ten, while an apprenticeship, depending upon the area of specialization, lasted from six to eight years.

The Arsenal was entirely surrounded by crenellated walls with only one land entrance, and the flow of persons entering and exiting was strictly controlled by the gate keepers in order to prevent theft. At night the doors were always closed and the area was continually patrolled by guards walking along the length of the walls. The sentinels called to each other every hour from the fifteen towers which punctuated the walls; when there was no response to two calls in a row, probably because a guard had fallen asleep, this latter was fired from his job. Beyond the walls, the area was densely populated by the families of the arsenalotti and by artisans involved in activities connected to the nearby naval shipyard. It was an intense and noisy scene, with workshops, laboratories and the warehouses of ironmongers, gunsmiths specialized in the welding of canon, manufacturers of shields, of shells, gun powder and the fabric for sails.

Entire buildings were given over to the fulfillment of precise tasks, such as the buil-

Facing page,
Vittore Carpaccio, Arrival
in Cologne, Stories from
the Life of St. Ursula, *1490.*
Gallerie dell'Accademia.
Precious example of a
Venetian ship built
at the Arsenal.

Following pages,
over the centuries the Istrian
stone portal was decorated
with lions, allegorical
sculptures and a statue
of Saint Giustina.

ding where the Historical Naval Museum now stands, which once housed the bakery for the production of biscuit bread, staple diet of crews. Another interesting example is the Marinarezza, a large residential complex characterized by two wide arch-like openings, which once contained fifty-five apartments for use by disabled sailors or those who had been commended for special services rendered to the Republic.

Access to the Arsenal by land is right next to the sea entrance and is an important portal of Renaissance style, perhaps the work of Antonio Gambello.

Over the years, it has undergone modifications and interesting additions, often in relation to historical events.

A case in point is the statue of S. Giustina, erected at the top of the door in 1571 to celebrate the victorious battle of Lepanto that had taken place precisely on that saint's day. In the following century, instead, was added the overlooking terracing, decorated with allegorical sculptures. Within the same time period, the daring Venetian admiral Francesco Morosini, who had bombed the Parthenon, returned following the reconquest of the Peloponese with a few trophies of war, among which the ancient lions that flanked the door. Beside the land entrance, there is one of the "water entrances", crowned by two imposing towers and crossed by a canal that connects the Arsenal to the basin of St. Mark's. Today the canal is still spanned by a wooden bridge that appears to be very similar to the original (which however was a drawbridge that allowed ships to pass through).

This corner of the city can also be seen in a painting by Canaletto in which the only clear difference is a small Doric temple dedicated to the Madonna that today no longer exists. On the right of the land entrance are two private bridges which, in remembrance of Dante's visit, were named *del Purgatorio* (of Purgatory) and *dell'Inferno* (of Hell), while another bridge on the left is called *del Paradiso* (of Paradise). The Arsenal's decline commenced in the second half of the 17th century: the English, French and Dutch fleets gradually ousted those of Venice, whether for political reasons (geographical discoveries had altered trade routes) or because of technical supremacy.

Following the French invasion, at the end of the 18th century, the Arsenal's activity significantly diminished, even if its infrastructure was periodically used for decades, up until the second World War. The building currently belongs to the Marina Militare of Venice.

In the last few years, many offers have been made to reuse its splendid spaces that preserve, in their impressiveness and in the silence which surrounds them, a unique charm. In the last two decades, a section of the ancient buildings has come to be well known by the general public as it has periodically been used by the Biennial of Venice for exhibitions of contemporary art and architecture and the production of theatre and dance shows.

ISLANDS

The elongated shape of Venice's lagoon stretches over an area of almost six hundred square kilometers, a little more than half of which consists of land above water. It is enclosed and protected from the sea by four strips of land: Lido, Cavallino, Chioggia and Pellestrina. Three port mouths allow the inflow of sea water and the consequent outflow of debris, ensuring the preservation of the lagoon. Over the centuries, man's constant and vigilant intervention, to offset continuous work of nature, has proven essential in safeguarding island populations and in enabling the development of the Serenissima. As early as the 16th century, Venetians had begun to divert the course of tributaries to prevent the deposited sediment from slowly filling the waters of the lagoon Two centuries later, part of the coast was consolidated by constructing the Murazzi, made of Istrian stone and pozzolana, to prevent erosion of the banks by the sea.

Following the review of many different projects to try to stem the problem of high tides, and after years of controversy, the *Mose* system is currently being built. Its effectiveness, and the extent of its impact on the environment, are still the cause of heated debate. The insidious waters around Venice, which in the past had often deterred enemies from penetrating, are still difficult to navigate today for those who are not familiar with the area. As it is difficult to navigate in the lagoon between the shallows and the sandbanks, navigable canals are marked by *bricole*, sets of three poles joined to one another to form a pyramid.

In addition to the great archipelago in the shape of a fish that is the city of Venice itself, the lagoon is dotted with many other islands of various sizes, each with its own history. Many of the smaller islands once housed Benedictine monasteries, centers of prayer and study where important manuscripts and works of art were collected and stored. Over time, many of the islands became places of treatment or convalescence, such as the Lazzaretto Vecchio where the contagious sick were confined, the Lazzaretto Nuovo which housed victims of the plague or Sacca Sessola for sufferers of tuberculosis. In more recent times specialized structures for the mentally ill were built on the islands of San Servolo and San Clemente, now housing respectively an international university and a luxurious hotel, while Isola delle Grazie, where until a few years ago infectious diseases were treated, has now been completely abandoned. The largest island of the lagoon is the Lido, a thin strip of land twelve kilometers long, long used for military purposes and for target shooting exercises with the crossbow. There stood the old church of S. Nicolò where a popular part

Facing page,
the island of San Giorgio
Maggiore bears the mark of
Palladio's architecture,
with its atmosphere of peace
and tranquility.

of *Festa della Sensa* took place, namely the "wedding with the sea". On this occasion annually on Ascension Day, the *Bucintoro*, the precious state vessel used for ceremonies, would set sail across the lagoon towards the sea. On board were the Doge, senior judges, foreign ambassadors and other prominent personalities, followed by thousands of vessels of all types. Having crossed the mouths of the port and reached the sea, the head of state would throw a ring into the water as a symbol of unity, saying the words: "We marry you, oh sea, as a symbol of true and ever-lasting dominion." There then followed a break for the religious ritual in S. Nicolò at the Lido, after which festivities began in earnest, lasting two weeks and culminating in St. Mark's Square, where temporary grandiose structures were set up to house the fair of local products. The tradition of the marriage with the sea continues today and it is the mayor of Venice who celebrates the traditional festival. The island of the Lido, inhabited only in relatively recent times, and more precisely since the mid 19th century, in time became a famous seaside resort. In the early years of the 20th century it reached the peak of its fame with the construction of magnificent hotels frequented by members of high society from the whole of Europe, such as the Excelsior and the Hotel Des Bains. Together with the imaginative Art Nouveau buildings, constructed in the same period, they bestowed upon the island an aura of elegance and sophistication. Today, the Lido is populated by a large number of residents and is still the beach area used by Venetians, with its beach facilities characterized by colorful huts that are rented for the summer. Formed from a small group of islands and known throughout the world for its traditional production of glass, Murano, like Venice, is crossed by a large main canal. In the 11th century, it was already a thriving city and was economically independent, to the point where it could count on a degree of autonomy from the capital which allowed the people of Murano to have their own laws and governors. The island had its moment of greatest splendor during the Renaissance numbered almost thirty thousand inhabitants, half of the current population of the entire lagoon. Murano was also a holiday resort for Venetians who owned sumptuous homes with lush gardens, the scene of leisure and literary circles. Evidence of glass production dates from the early 11th century, but it was only in the 13th century that the statute of the corporation of glaziers came into force to regulate such activities, conferring to it protection guaranteed by the state. Also, at the same time it was decided to move all of the furnaces from Venice to Murano to limit potential fire damage. The concentration of all glass producers in this location led to an increase in activity across the island. The quality of Murano glass was a guarantee which made it a coveted product. Orders were received from many different places, thereby attracting to the lagoon a large and constant flow of money. For this reason the glaziers were subjected to strict rules which, for example, forbade them from moving out of town, so that they wouldn't divulge the precious secrets of the profession. Penalties for those who did not adhere to regulations ranged from seizure of property to the death penalty. On the other hand, the category enjoyed concrete protection from the State which brought several advantages. A significant privilege granted to glaziers was that their daughters were entitled to marry nobles, a rather exceptional concession given the separation of castes in Venetian society. The glass products created by Murano's glass furnaces have always been both functional and decorative: this vast production includes chandeliers, mirrors, vases and glasses. Many of the ancient techniques are still employed, including hot applications, *fili-*

grana a reticello (colorless and opaque white glass with a netlike pattern of threads), *incalmo* (multi strata colored glass), cladding, etching, *millefiori* (produced from canes of colored glass that are fused together and cut crosswise) and *murrine*. For centuries Murano glass production was unthreatened by foreign competition, except in the 18th century when fine glass from England and Bohemia began to invade the international market. Having overcome competition from the north, today the kilns suffer more from the competition of Chinese imitations, characterized by lower prices and decidedly poor quality. A wonderful testimony of the ancient glories of Murano is represented by the basilica of S. Donato, one of the oldest churches in the lagoon. Built in Venetian-Byzantine style in the 12th century, it features an exterior hexagonal apse sustained over two tiers marked by blind arches supported by white columns. The superb mosaic floor is rich in ornamental motifs and symbolic representations of animals that transport the visitor into a distant, legendary world. The island of Burano, a small fisherman's area, enjoys international fame, especially due to the famous production of lace which still flourishes today.

Crossed by small canals teeming with boats, in addition to fondamenta (banks), campi (squares) and calli (narrow alleys) where one can still see fishing nets drying in the sun, the island is notable for its simple houses with gaudy colors. Each household chooses a particular color for its home and if two families live together, the building is painted in two different colors. The art of lace originated in the 16th century. Initially it was a pastime to which nuns devoted themselves in the silence of the

In the monastery at San Lazzaro degli Armeni are stored more than 100,000 volumes.

Currently the home of an
international university,
San Servolo had once been the
site of a psychiatric
hospital.

convents, or an activity undertaken by no-
blewomen during long days spent inside
their homes. As lace became an indispen-
sable accessory in women's fashion, demand progressively grew, creating a profession within its own right, at which the
women of Burano excelled. For almost
two centuries lace was the main source of
income for the island, which prospered
through the export of its products, sought
after by ladies across Europe. Torcello was
one of the first islands to be inhabited by
populations fleeing the barbarian inva-

sions. In the 7th century, the bishop of Al-
tino, a rich Roman center in the hinter-
land, moved there with his entourage. For
almost five centuries the island was one of
the most important of the lagoon, due to
the merchant and port activities confident
in their competitive position. The thriving
economy led to the development of com-
prehensive urban planning. In addition to
housing, at least seven churches, a number
of monasteries and other important buildings were built, with the incorporation of
Roman fragments taken from the hinter-

Following pages,
the basilica of San Donato
in Murano was built
in the Venetian-Byzantine
style, and is one of the oldest
churches in the lagoon.

land. The economic activity of residents gradually slowed due to the natural filling of the surrounding waters. Over time, these areas became swamps and prevented ships from entering the port. The stagnant water also proved to fatal to residents as it caused the spread of malaria. Around the 12th century, deteriorating economic and health conditions forced the population to relocate to nearby islands or to Venice, where the port of Rivo Alto (Rialto) was preparing to become one of most important European ports. A small core of Tor-

cello's historic structure remains today, forming part of the cathedral of S. Maria Assunta, the oldest of the lagoon, the church of S. Fosca and the baptistery of S. Maria Assunta preserves the morphology of the first Christian temples, with a basilica plan, with three naves separated by two colonnades and owes its elegance to the simplicity and rhythm of the play of light and shadow that unravels from the columns up to the altar. The focal point is the apse, entirely covered with golden mosaics of Byzantine style. Alongside stands the

The church of San Michele in Isola, designed by Mauro Codussi, was the first work in the Renaissance style to appear on the waters of the lagoon.

ancient baptistery, built in the traditional circular shape, while the church of S. Fosca, built around the 12th century – perhaps as a shrine for the relics of martyrs – is based on a central plan defined externally by an octagonal porch. A contemporary interpretation governs the function of these three religious monuments: the baptistery is the symbol of nascent life which leads to the cathedral, symbolic of life in progress, arriving at S. Fosca, a symbol of death, which, through martyrdom, leads to life after death.

A more recent structure is that of San Lazzaro degli Armeni, an ancient Benedictine settlement whose church dates from the 14th century. The island later became a hospital for lepers and then a haven for beggars, until the beginning of the 18th century, when the Venetian Republic transferred the area to a community of Armenian monks, who transformed it into one of the major centers of Armenian culture. Relations between Venetians and Armenians date from the 13th century, when the latter were given the opportunity to own an inn and a church located in Calle degli Armeni, not far from St. Mark's Square. The Armenians in the city were mostly merchants and craftsmen specialized in the trade of silk and precious stones from Persia, and were esteemed guests due to their industrious quality and their ability to bring profits to the Serenissima. The Armenian monastery was governed by strict discipline based on the study and learning of the

technique of printing. The Armenian printing press was one of the most famous of
the 18th century, attracted writers from all
over the world, including Lord Byron, an
assiduous frequenter of San Lazzaro. The
laboratory has not been active for decades
but the island still hosts the offices of the
publisher. The valuable library, still open,
holds 100,000 books and more than 3,000
manuscripts. The Armenian fathers also
own the splendid Palazzo Zenobio in Venice, until recently the site of a college for
deserving young Armenians. On the other
hand, the island of Lazzaretto Vecchio,
which since 1249 and for nearly a century
was the location of a community of Hermit
Fathers, endured considerable pain and
suffering. The island was known to the pil-

grims who during their travels to the Holy
Land could stop and receive hospitality by
the monks in this large monastery. During
the following century, as a result of a government order, the area became an asy-
lum for people suffering from contagious
diseases. After being turned into a military
garrison in the 19th century, the island fell
into a state of neglect. In ancient times the
Lazzaretto was formed from two islands
connected by a bridge. A gunpowder factory stood on the smaller island, while the
hospital itself was located on the larger island, and was built by incorporating the
existing convent of Santa Maria di Nazareth. The term *lazzaretto*, used to define
the place where the contagious sick were
confined, probably derives from the cor-

*The church of Santa Fosca
in Torcello has a circular plan
and is defined externally by an
octagonal portico.*

ruption of the word "Nazareth". Subsequently, the word Vecchio, meaning old, was added to the name to distinguish it from the island of Lazzaretto Nuovo (new) where a shelter for victims of the plague was established in the 15th century.

The terrible plague endured for centuries as the scourge of the entire known world. As a port city, Venice was not spared by the devastating infection, which deeply upset the rhythm and equilibrium of everday life. Every epidemic killed tens of thousands of citizens, their numbers quickly replaced by foreigners who, attracted by the mirage of the capital, settled in, bringing stimuli and new energy. Three major plagues swept through Venice, each one wiping out up to one-third of the population: the plague of 1348 (the infamous Black Death), that of 1575 and finally the epidemic of 1630. At that time the Venetians were not able to defend themselves from disease because they were unaware of its origin and causes. Today we know that infection was spread through the fleas of infected rats which travelled to Venice in the holds of ships that arrived from the East, but at the time, doctors crafted the most imaginative theories and assumptions. It was thought for example that contamination came from the air, in the mephitic miasma of the winds which were absorbed by the skin and lungs, or was related to the range of lowest and highest temperatures occurring in a 24-hour time span, or resulted from unfavorable astral cycles. Recommended precautions included burning aromatic wood at home, the use of amulets, healing herbs and stones, and leaving one's home only at night with a vinegar-infused sponge placed under the nose. Bleedings and purges, a common remedy during those times, were also recommended. The swellings were cut into and after the suspected poison was removed, were cauterized with red-hot irons. There were also special recipes such as eating a fig and a walnut in the morning to fasting for several days or spreading a special healing oil on the wrists. In the first half of the 15th century, it was established that patients were to be hospitalized on certain islands and the government made an explicit request for its citizens to leave in their wills funds to be used for the construction of hospitals. A second major hospital was built on the island and was eventually given the name of Lazzaretto Nuovo. It could accommodate up to 4,000 recovering patients or suspected cases in quarantine. Once it was understood that the spread of the plague was caused by the movement of people and objects, ships were confined out of the port and contact with the plague-ridden area was forbidden. Crew and cargo were put into quarantine on the island of Lazzaretto Nuovo, where some buildings still remain along with a well and the ancient walls. In one of the buildings, one can still observe the drawings and simple inscriptions made by sailors held in quarantine, which refer to love, travel and distant ports. The island of Lazzaretto Nuovo is now under protection as public civic property. A different way of life animated the island of San Giorgio Maggiore. Sitting across the water from St. Mark's Square, the island bears the mark of the skilled Andrea Palladio with his grand church design, and the buildings and the adjacent cloisters, pervaded by an atmosphere of peace and spirituality. In ancient times, it was one of the richest monasteries in the lagoon and housed a collection of rare books and works of art.

At the beginning of the 19th century, Napoleon suppressed the religious community and dispersed its treasures, but a cleric managed to stay in the rooms previously inhabited by monks and continued to live there.

This allowed the subsequent rebuilding of the Benedictine community, which now lives side by side with the cultural activities

of Fondazione Giorgio Cini. Many other islands dot the lagoon of Venice, each with a distinct appperarance, history and function: the island of San Michele which, since the mid-19th century, accommodates the cemetery of the Venetians; Sant'Erasmo and Vignole, known as the 'gardens of the lagoon'; and San Francesco del Deserto, which still retains its ancient monastic calling. Other smaller islands have become privately owned or will be sold at auction (as has already been the case in the past).

The church of San Clemente, on the island by the same name, has a Renaissance façade in Istrian stone and faces east.

Following pages, view of of a campo on the island of Burano, with the typical brightly-colored houses.

BIBLIOGRAPHY

G. ALDEGANI, *Le corti. Spazi pubblici e privati nella città di Venezia*, Milano, Citta-Studi 1991

G. BELLAVITIS, *L'Arsenale di Venezia. Storia di una grande struttura urbana*, Venezia, Marsilio, 1983

Storia della civiltà veneziana, a cura di V. BRANCA, 11 voll., Firenze, Sansoni 1955-65

R. CALIMANI, *Storia del ghetto di Venezia*, Milano, Mondandori, 1995

E. CONCINA, *Le chiese di Venezia. L'arte e la storia*, Udine, Magnus, 1995

E. CONCINA, *Storia dell'architettura di Venezia. Dal VII al XX secolo,* Milano, Electa, 1995

E. CONCINA, *L'Arsenale della Repubblica di Venezia*, Milano, Electa, 1984

M. CUNICO, *Il giardino veneziano. La storia, l'architettura, la botanica*, Venezia, Albrizzi, 1989

P. FORTINI BROWN, *Private Lives in Renaissance Venice. Art, Architecture, and the Family*, New Haven-London, Yale University Press, 2004

P. FORTINI BROWN, *Art and Life in Renaissance Venice,* New York, Abrams, 1997

P. FORTINI BROWN, *Venetian Narrative Painting in the Age of Carpaccio*, New Haven, Yale University Press, 1988

R. J. GOY, *Venice. The City and its Architecture*, London, Phaidon, 1997

R. J. GOY, *Venetian Vernacular Architecture. Traditional Housing in the Venetian Lagoon*, Cambridge, Cambridge University Press, 1989

A. HOPKINS, *Santa Maria della Salute. Architecture and Ceremony in Baroque Venice*, Cambridge, Cambridge University Press, 2000

D. HOWARD, *The Architectural History of Venice*, New Haven-London, Yale University Press, 2002

P. HUMPHREY, *Painting in Renaissance Venice*, New Haven-London, Yale University Press, 1995

F.C. LANE, *Venice. A Maritime Republic,* Baltimore, Johns Hopkins University Press, 1973

F.C. LANE, *Venetian Ships and Shipbuilders of the Renaissance*, Baltimore, The Johns Hopkins Press, 1934

G. LORENZETTI, *Venezia e il suo estuario. Guida storico-artistica*, Roma, Istituto Poligrafico dello Stato, Libreria dello Stato, 1956

G. MAZZUCCO, *Monasteri benedettini nella laguna veneziana,* Venezia, Arsenale, 1983

G. MAZZUCCO, *Guida alle Magistrature. Elementi per la conoscenza della Repubblica Veneta,* a cura di C. MILAN

P. MOLMENTI, *La storia di Venezia nella vita privata dalle origini alla caduta della Repubblica,* 4 voll., Bergamo, Istituto Italiano d'Arti Grafiche, 1905-08

E. MUIR, *Civic Ritual in Renaissance Venice,* Princeton, Princeton University Press, 1981

G. PAVANELLO e G. ROMANELLI, *Venezia nell'Ottocento: immagini e mito,* Electa, 1983

G. PEROCCO e A. SALVADORI, *Civiltà di Venezia,* 3 voll., Venezia, Stamperia di Venezia, 1973

Le Scuole di Venezia, a cura di T. PIGNATTI, Milano, Electa, 1981

T. PIGNATTI, *L'arte veneziana,* Venezia, Arsenale, 1989

H. PIRENNE, *Maometto e Carlomagno,* Roma-Bari, Laterza, 1992

U. PIZZARELLO, *Pietre e legni dell'Arsenale di Venezia,* Venezia, L'altra riva, 1983

A. POLITI, B. VIANELLO, Verona, Cierre, 2003

B. PULLAN, *La politica sociale della Repubblica di Venezia 1500-1620,* Volume I: *Le Scuole Grandi, l'assistenza e la legge sui poveri,* Roma, Il Veltro, 1982

A. RIZZI, *I leoni di San Marco. Il simbolo della Repubblica veneta nella scultura e nella pittura,* Venezia, Arsenale, 2001

T. RIZZO, *I ponti di Venezia. Una romantica passeggiata nella intelaiatura, unica al mondo, di calle, rii e canali. Personaggi storici e leggendari, maschere e feste dell'antica tradizione veneziana rivivono nell'incanto magico della laguna,* Roma, Newton Compton, 1983

J. SCHULZ, *The New Palaces of Medieval Venice,* University Park, Pennsylvania State University Press, 2004

G. TASSINI, *Curiosità veneziane, ovvero origini delle denominazioni stradali,* Venezia, Filippi, 1964

E.R. TRINCANATO, *Venezia minore,* Venezia, Filippi, 1972

Il giardino veneto. Dal tardo Medioevo al Novecento, a cura di M. AZZI VISENTINI, Milano, Electa, 1988

G. ZALIN, *Dalla bottega alla fabbrica. La fenomenologia industriale nelle province venete tra '500 e '900,* Verona, Libreria Universitaria Editrice, 1992

A. ZORZI, *La Repubblica del Leone. Storia di Venezia,* Milano, Bompiani, 2002

G. ZUCCHETTA, *Venezia, ponte per ponte. "vita, morte e miracoli" dei 443 manufatti che attraversano i canali della città,* Venezia, Stamperia di Venezia, 1992

Venezia e la peste. 1348-1797, Venezia, Marsilio, 1980

PHOTOGRAPH CREDITS

Andrea Darra: pp. 72, 75, 76-77, 90-91, 95, 108, 109, 114-115, 123, 128-129, 136, 140, 141, 144-145, 146, 168-169, 171

Archivio Arsenale, Venezia: pp. 6, 9, 13, 15, 19, 22, 23, 26, 27, 29-30, 33, 37, 39, 40, 42, 43, 47-48, 50-51, 52-53, 57, 58-59, 60, 61, 63, 64-65, 67, 68-69, 74, 78, 79, 82, 88, 89, 93, 96-97, 100-101, 105, 106-107, 110-111, 116, 119, 133, 134-135, 137, 138, 142, 148, 149, 151. 152, 153, 154, 155, 156-157, 158, 172-173, 174, 186-187

Archivio Scala, Firenze: pp. 54, 70, 86, 102, 130

Luciano Romano: pp. 16-17, 28-29, 34-35, 45, 49, 73, 83, 84, 85, 143, 180-181, 182, 183

Magistrato alle acque di Venezia: pp. 177, 178-179, 185

Mark E. Smith: pp. 20, 24, 81, 99, 120-121, 124-125, 127, 139, 160, 161, 162-163, 164, 165, 167

The publisher apologizes in advance if, for reasons beyond his control, any source was omitted or cited inaccurately.

Printed
in October 2012
by EBS Editoriale Bortolazzi-Stei S.r.l.
San Giovanni Lupatoto (Verona) - Italy